Choosing the President

Also by The League of Women Voters

Choosing the President

A Citizen's Guide to the 2000 Election

The League of Women Voters

The Lyons Press

Copyright © 1999 by the League of Women Voters

Printed in Canada
Design by Compset, Inc.

10   9   8   7   6   5   4   3   2

Library of Congress Cataloging-in-Publication Data

Choosing the president : a citizen's guide to the 2000 election/
   The League of Women Voters.
       p.   cm.
   Includes bibliographical references and index.
   ISBN 1-55821-959-5 (pb)   ISBN 1-55821-958-7 (hc)
     1. Presidents—United States—Election.   2. Voting—United States.
   3. Electioneering—United States.   4. Presidential candidates—
   United States.   5. Elections—United States.   I. League of Women
   Voters (U.S.)
   JK528.C43   1999
   324.6'3'0973—dc21   99-23839
                                                          CIP

Contents

Acknowledgments

Choosing the President 2000 was written for the League of Women Voters Education Fund by William H. Woodwell, Jr., a Washington, DC–area writer and editorial consultant. This completely rewritten edition is part of a proud League tradition of providing a step-by-step guide to the process by which we choose our presidents. Earlier editions of *Choosing the President* go back more than ten presidential election cycles. The League and the writer gratefully acknowledge the preparers of those earlier editions. This edition builds particularly on the 1984 edition published by the League of Women Voters Education Fund and the 1992 edition published by the League of Women Voters of California Education Fund.

Major revisions for *Choosing the President 2000* were made to reflect the tremendous changes in the way the presidential election is experienced by voters at the dawn of the twenty-first century. While the constitutional process of choosing the president remains much as it has been for more than two hundred years, the context in which it takes place would be unrecognizable to voters of earlier generations. Communications technology, campaign finance, political strategy, and voter behavior are just some of the factors influencing the way the presidential campaign unfolds today. The simplification of the text and the reorganization of the book into two parts, "The Players" and "The Process," are designed to help readers put all of the pieces together in an easy-to-understand way.

We are grateful to all those who contributed to this edition and to earlier editions, to League members and other volunteers across the country who provide accessible information and services to voters, and especially to all Americans who participate in choosing the president.

Introduction

The United States presidential election is the biggest event in American politics. It is an exciting and complicated process that begins immediately after the preceding election and doesn't end until you, the voter, have your say.

What happens in between is a campaign not just for votes but for political contributions, favorable media coverage, endorsements from celebrities and party leaders, and all the other makings of a winning candidacy for the highest elected office in the land. Key events along the way include the primaries and caucuses, the party conventions, and the debates—not to mention all the speeches, the polls, the focus groups, and the barrage of radio and television commercials imploring you to vote this way or that.

It's easy to get overwhelmed. And that's why the League of Women Voters produced this book. Trying to follow the presidential election without an understanding of what's going on and why is like watching a foreign-language film without the subtitles. You may get a general idea about the plot and characters, but you'll miss out on what's really happening. You'll miss a lot of the drama and excitement as well.

The presidential election process is constantly evolving. The advent of television, the increasing role of money in politics, an accelerated schedule of primary elections, and declining voter interest are just a few of the recent developments that have transformed the way we choose the president.

In the pages that follow, you'll learn more about these and many other topics. This book doesn't tell you how to vote. But it does try to explain why certain things happen the way they do—for example, why the campaigning starts so early, why the political parties have less control over the process than they used to, why money is so important, and why the candidates focus so intently on winning certain states.

Choosing the President also offers pointers for getting the most out of the election by directing you to the best political Web sites, helping you evaluate news coverage, and suggesting what to look for when watching the debates and the conventions and when trying to make sense of all the polls and the television and radio ads.

This book was created to provide a handy and accessible overview of the presidential election process *while it is happening* in the weeks and months leading up to the November 2000 election. It can be read from cover to cover or picked up as needed when you want to know more about what's happening, or about something in the news.

A presidential election is your opportunity to shape this country's future and have a say on important issues that affect your life. With a better understanding of what's involved in choosing the president, you'll be better equipped to follow the campaign more closely, and better able to make an informed decision come November.

—League of Women Voters

PART I

The Players

We the People

The most important players in the election of a United States president are not the candidates or their staffs, not the political parties or the other organizations with a stake in the outcome, and not the media pundits who make a habit of trying to tell us what we think. No, as hard as it is to remember sometimes, a presidential election revolves around the beliefs and the actions of American voters. Come Election Day, no one else's opinions matter, and no one else has control over the outcome.

Voting is the great equalizer in American society. No matter how much money you have or who your friends are or whether or not you contributed to a particular candidate, you have one vote—the same as everybody else. And with that one vote, you have the power to affect decisions that will affect your life. Your job, your taxes, your health care, your children's education, your Social Security, you name it—they are all at stake.

It's Been a Long Road: Voting in the Nation's Early Years

Today, every American age eighteen and older has the right to vote. Sometimes it's a right we take for granted. We forget how much hard work and how much blood, sweat, and tears have gone into expanding the franchise, or making sure that all segments of the American population—minorities, women, youth, and others—are able to have their say.

Despite their opposition to arbitrary rule and their faith in popular sovereignty, the United States' founders did not have in mind that all adults should be able to vote. During the early years of the country's history, legislatures in the United States generally restricted voting to white males who were twenty-one years of age or older. Many states also limited voting rights to those who "had a stake in society." Translation: to vote you had to own property. State governments began to eliminate the property requirement during the 1820s and 1830s.

By the time of the Civil War, almost all states had broadened the right to vote to all adult free males, property owners or not; black males had won the right to vote in most Northern states. In the decades since, the power base of American democracy has gradually widened, moving the nation closer and closer to the vision set forth in the Declaration of Independence of a government that derives its power from "the consent of the governed."

Opening Democracy's Door: Expanding the Franchise

The U.S. Constitution left it to the states to determine precisely who was qualified to vote. As a result, expanding voting rights to Americans who had been turned away or discouraged from voting has required either: (1) a constitutional amendment to make it the law of the land that certain groups cannot be denied the right to vote; or (2) changes in federal law to remove barriers to registration and voting and to make it easier for all Americans to have their say.

To this day, the states still set the basic qualifications for voting, but they may not turn away certain categories of people, thanks to a series of constitutional amendments:

- The Fifteenth Amendment, ratified in 1870, ensured that Americans could not be denied the right to vote on account of their race. The amendment was one of three that were ratified in the Reconstruction era following the Civil War in an effort to ensure equal rights for African-Americans. The other Reconstruction amendments were the Thirteenth, which outlawed slavery, and the Fourteenth, which guaranteed equal protection under the law for all citizens, regardless of their race.

- The Nineteenth Amendment, ratified in 1920, marked the end of a decades-long struggle for equal voting rights for women. By 1916, women were able to vote in only twelve states; the vast majority of American women still were denied this fundamental right. In the end, the fight for women's voting rights was led by the National American Woman Suffrage Association, the precursor to today's League of Women Voters.

- The Twenty-sixth Amendment is the most recent constitutional amendment relating to the right to vote. Ratified in 1971, it extended the vote to anyone eighteen years of age and over. Until then, states had generally restricted voting to the twenty-one-and-over population.

Other constitutional amendments have expanded the electorate in different ways—with the Twenty-third (ratified in 1961) allowing residents of the District of Columbia to vote for president, and the Twenty-fourth (1964) outlawing the poll

Constitutional Amendments Expanding the Right to Vote

AMENDMENT XV, Section 1. The right of citizens of the United States to vote shall not be denied or abridged by the United States or by any State on account of race, color, or previous condition of servitude. *(Ratified in 1870)*

AMENDMENT XIX, Section 1. The right of citizens of the United States to vote shall not be denied or abridged by the United States or by any State on account of sex. *(Ratified in 1920)*

AMENDMENT XXIV, Section 1. The right of citizens of the United States to vote in any primary or other election for President or Vice President, for electors for President or Vice President, or for Senator or Representative in Congress, shall not be denied or abridged by the United States or any State by reason of failure to pay any poll tax or other tax. *(Ratified in 1964)*

AMENDMENT XXVI, Section 1. The right of citizens of the United States, who are eighteen years of age or older, to vote shall not be denied or abridged by the United States or by any State on account of age. *(Ratified in 1971)*

taxes that discouraged poor people, mostly African-Americans, from voting in many Southern states. It is hard to believe today, but poll taxes meant that people actually had to pay to vote.

Together, these constitutional changes have had the effect of legally extending the eligibility to vote to all United States citizens over eighteen years of age, with the exception in most states of convicted felons.

Unfinished Business: Lowering the Barriers to Voting

The fact that the Constitution told states they couldn't deny certain groups the right to vote didn't keep states from erecting barriers to registration and voting—barriers that ensured that certain groups would be underrepresented at the polls.

In the late nineteenth century, in fact, many Southern states tried to get around the Fifteenth Amendment's guarantee of equal voting rights for blacks by adding grandfather clauses to their state constitutions. These clauses generally limited the right to vote to those individuals who had been able to vote before the Fifteenth Amendment became law, along with their descendants. The Supreme Court declared these laws unconstitutional in the early twentieth century.

Poll taxes were an early example of the other barriers facing African Americans and other minorities seeking to exercise their right to vote. Over the years, states also have used literacy tests and English-language requirements, length-of-residency requirements, and onerous voter-registration rules to keep registration and voting rates down among racial and ethnic minorities, the poor, and other groups.

In recent decades, two major pieces of federal legislation have sought to break down these and other barriers to registration and voting: the Voting Rights Act, originally enacted in 1965; and the National Voter Registration Act, signed into law in 1993.

THE VOTING RIGHTS ACT

The Voting Rights Act is a complex and detailed law, but its basic goal is to make sure that racial minorities, no matter where they live, have the same opportunity as other citizens to participate in the nation's political life. The law was enacted to try to stop some of the common practices that restricted African-American voting in many Southern states.

Passage of the Voting Rights Act happened shortly after civil rights activists organized a protest march in Selma, Alabama, in March 1965 with the goal of drawing national attention to the struggle for black voting rights. Violence erupted as police brutally attacked the marchers on a day that came to be known as Bloody Sunday. Another march was organized two weeks later and culminated in an address by the Reverend Martin Luther King, Jr., that drew twenty thousand people to the state capital of Montgomery. The episode created new support for the Voting Rights Act, which President Lyndon Johnson signed into law that August.

The following are some of the law's key provisions:

- No citizen can be prevented from voting in presidential elections because of length-of-residency requirements
- No one can deny an eligible citizen the right to vote or interfere with or intimidate anyone seeking to register to vote

- Literacy tests and other methods cannot be used as qualifications for voting in any federal, state, local, general, or primary election
- Seven states and a number of local jurisdictions with a historical pattern of discrimination based on race must submit any changes in their election laws to the U.S. Justice Department for approval.

In 1975, Congress added provisions to the act to make sure that United States citizens are not deprived of the right to vote because they cannot read, write, or speak English. Another series of amendments in 1982 provided that Americans with disabilities cannot be prohibited from bringing someone else to the polls to help them vote, so long as that person is not the voter's employer or union representative.

But even with the Voting Rights Act and its additional provisions on the books, minorities and other groups still faced difficulties in registration and voting well into the 1990s. Intimidating threats, patronizing treatment at registration and polling places, and poor service to minority registrants still were widely reported.

In many states, the law required citizens to appear in person during weekday hours to register to vote, overlooking the fact that large numbers of residents—many of them lower-income, hourly workers—couldn't get away from their jobs. In addition, some election officials refused to allow minority organizations to help run voter-registration drives. This may not have been blatant discrimination, but it was clear that many local and state officials still considered voting a privilege and not a right.

THE NATIONAL VOTER REGISTRATION ACT

From 1970 through the early 1990s, Congress considered a number of proposals aimed at eliminating the remaining hurdles to registration and voting. But these measures generally failed because senators and representatives in Washington tended to shy away from dictating how the states should run federal elections. Also, members of Congress were no doubt reluctant to change a system that had worked to get them elected.

In 1992, however, after a multiyear campaign by voter-registration-reform advocates from such organizations as the League of Women Voters and the NAACP, both houses of Congress finally passed a law making voter registration easier and more convenient. The National Voter Registration Act required states to allow citizens to apply to register to vote when they get their driver's licenses. The law also required states to offer mail-in voter registration and registration at offices offering public assistance. President George Bush vetoed the law, however, and it was left to the next Congress to revisit the issue in 1993.

Registration Increases After Passage of Motor Voter Law		
	1992	1996
Number of Voters Registered	133.8 million	149.8 million
Percentage of Voting-Age Population	70.6 percent	76.25 percent

With a new president in the White House who supported voter-registration reform, members of Congress reintroduced the legislation—also known as "motor voter"—and delivered it for President Bill Clinton's signature in May 1993. Clinton's statement at the signing ceremony placed the new law in the context of the centuries-old fight for universal voting rights:

> *The victory we celebrate today is but the most recent chapter in the overlapping struggles of our nation's history to enfranchise women and minorities, the disabled and the young, with the power to affect their own destiny, and our common destiny, by participating fully in our democracy.*

The National Voter Registration Act took effect in most states on January 1, 1995. By the time of the 1996 presidential election, the number of registered voters in the United States had reached an all-time high, comprising more than 76 percent of the voting-age population. According to the Federal Election Commission (FEC), the surge in registrations in 1995 and 1996 was primarily due to the motor voter law.

Motor Voter Under Fire

Despite its success in increasing voter registration throughout the country, opponents have continued to criticize the National Voter Registration Act. Between 1994 and 1998, critics on Capitol Hill offered legislation to repeal the law, to require proof of citizenship and Social Security numbers on registration applications, and to drop voters from the rolls simply for not voting. All of these efforts failed.

Turnout Turns Down: Voter Participation Hits New Low

With more people eligible to vote and voter registration rates on the rise, you'd think that the percentage of Americans showing up at the polls would be higher than ever. But that's not the case.

Although more people vote in presidential elections than in any other American elections, even this biggest contest in American politics has been a victim of declining voter interest. In November 1996, less than half of eligible Americans showed up at the polls to vote for Bill Clinton, Bob Dole, Ross Perot, or another presidential candidate. It was the lowest voter turnout on record for a presidential contest, and it continued a downward trend that started in 1960, when more than six out of ten Americans turned out in an election that sent John F. Kennedy to the White House.

One of the most disturbing implications of the declining turnout figures, according to many observers, is that a relatively small proportion of the American electorate now has the power to determine who is president. Just 26 percent of the voting-age population elected George Bush in 1988, and Bill Clinton was reelected in 1996 with the support of only 23 percent of all eligible voters. When only one out of four Americans are deciding who's president, it leaves the door wide open to the election of a president who doesn't necessarily reflect the will or the priorities of the American public.

In other countries around the world, voter turnout rates are often much higher than in the United States. According to the FEC, countries with high levels of voter participation in recent presidential and parliamentary elections include:

Voter Turnout in Presidential Elections, 1960–1996	
Year	Percentage of Voting-Age Population
1960	63
1964	62
1968	61
1972	55*
1976	54
1980	53
1984	53
1988	50
1992	55
1996	49

SOURCE: Congressional Research Service
*A likely factor in the significant decline in voter turnout between 1968 and 1972 was the ratification of the Twenty-sixth Amendment to the Constitution in 1971. The amendment expanded the right to vote to younger Americans (18–21 years of age), a group that historically has recorded low turnout rates when compared to other segments of the population.

Argentina (81 percent); Australia (96 percent); Canada (73 percent); the Czech Republic (76 percent); Ghana (78 percent); and Italy (77 percent).

Turning Things Around: How to Increase Voter Turnout

One possible response to decreasing levels of voter turnout in the United States is to improve American politics—that is, to compel the candidates and the political parties to focus more on the issues and less on the scripted, feel-good events, the thirty-second advertisements, and the negative appeals that dominate today's national political campaigns. Some of the proposals to change the way we pay for elections include provisions aimed in part at accomplishing this goal (see chapter 5).

But many people believe that major changes in the way political campaigns are run in the United States are about as likely as a comet striking Washington, D.C. In that case, perhaps the best way to try to turn around the turnout picture is to make sure voters have as much information as possible about the candidates and the issues, and about how the election will affect people's lives.

According to the League of Women Voters' own research, the degree to which people feel that the outcome of an election will affect them and their families has a lot to do with whether or not they vote. In other words, people need information that connects the election to what's happening at work, in their communities, and in their homes.

Getting election information has become a lot easier in recent years, thanks in great part to the Internet. But that doesn't mean the rest of the media are off the hook. In fact, many people believe newspapers, radio, and television can do a much better job of reporting on the issues and informing voters about what's at stake in elections (see chapter 4).

Yet another way to increase voter turnout, based on the League's survey findings, is for citizens to get involved in encouraging friends, family members, and coworkers to vote. In other words, Uncle Sam wants *you* to help increase voter turnout in this country. How can you help?

Register to Vote! It's Easier Than Ever

Thanks to the National Voter Registration Act, registering to vote is easier and more convenient than ever before. Now all states but four* must allow citizens to register to vote by mail and must accept a universal mail-in voter registration form designed by the Federal Election Commission. The form makes voter registration an easy, three-step process:

1. Get a mail-in voter registration form by calling your election office or the local League of Women Voters.
2. Complete the form according to the easy-to-follow instructions.
3. Mail the form to the address provided in the instructions.

The election office will notify you when your application has been approved and tell you where to go on election day to cast your ballot.

How else can I register? The motor voter law also requires states to make voter registration applications available in many public agencies where it was not available before. If you go to the department of motor vehicles to renew your driver's license, for example, your state has to offer you the opportunity to apply to register to vote at the same time that they are processing your driver's license renewal. Registration opportunities also must be made available at agencies that provide public assistance and services to people with disabilities. Last but not least, most states make forms available to the public in other locations, including libraries, schools, and the offices of the county clerk.

*Minnesota, North Dakota, Wyoming, and Wisconsin are exempt from the requirements of the motor voter law because: (1) they don't require registration at all; or (2) they allow voters to register at the polls on Election Day.

- Talk to people about the candidates and the issues and why you feel it's important to vote.
- Find out if your family, friends, and neighbors have what they need to make an informed decision and get to the polls. Maybe all they need is a ride.
- Don't go to the polling place alone. Make a date to take a friend.

A country where less than half the eligible population are counted on Election Day can hardly be called a true democracy. Do your part to help get out the vote!

The Candidates

The candidates, of course, are the star players in the presidential election. They get all the attention, and they select the issues they'll focus on and the messages they'll convey to voters. They also determine how their campaigns will be run—for example, how they'll go about their fund-raising, how many debates (if any) they'll participate in, whether they'll "go negative" in their advertising and other appeals, and how much information they'll provide about their policy positions and the specific things they'd do if elected.

The 2000 presidential election is the first since 1988 with no incumbent president in the race. The result is an open nomination contest in both the Democratic and Republican parties. Al Gore, as the sitting vice president, was presumed to have a leg up on any Democratic opponents in the early going, but his nomination was never a given; several prominent figures in his party were considering entering the race at one time or another.

Duties and Powers of the President

U.S. CONSTITUTION, ARTICLE II, Section 2. (1) The President shall be Commander in Chief of the Army and Navy of the United States, and of the Militia of the several States, when called into the actual Service of the United States; he may require the Opinion in writing, of the principal officer in each of the executive Departments, upon any subject relating to the Duties of their respective Offices, and he shall have Power to Grant Reprieves and Pardons for Offenses against the United States, except in Cases of Impeachment.

Section 2. (2) He shall have Power, by and with the Advice and Consent of the Senate, to make Treaties, provided two-thirds of the Senators present concur; and he shall nominate, and by and with the Advice and Consent of the Senate, shall appoint Ambassadors, other public Ministers and Consuls, Judges of the supreme Court, and all other Officers of the United States, whose Appointments are not herein otherwise provided for, and which shall be established by Law: but the Congress may by Law vest the Appointment of such inferior officers, as they think proper, in the President alone, in the Courts of Law, or in the Heads of Departments.

Section 3. He shall from time to time give to the Congress Information of the State of the Union, and recommend to their Consideration such Measures as he shall judge necessary and expedient; he may, on extraordinary Occasions, convene both Houses, or either of them, and in Case of Disagreement between them, with Respect to the Time of Adjournment, he may adjourn them to such Time as he shall think proper; he shall receive Ambassadors and other public Ministers; he shall take Care that the Laws be faithfully executed, and shall Commission all the Officers of the United States.

Are They Crazy? What It Takes to Run for President

A lot of people think that running for president in this day and age is a crazy thing to do. Not only must a candidate raise millions of dollars in contributions just to be a contender, but he or she has to give up a normal life for month after month of nonstop campaigning that can start as early as two years before the first primary. In addition, by entering a presidential race, a candidate and his or her family are exposed to an unprecedented level of scrutiny that can turn personal and family matters into headline stories, and can make past transgressions, however slight, into fodder for an opponents' negative appeals.

The number and variety of candidates who are vying for the presidency in 2000, however, prove that for many the attraction of serving in the White House still trumps concerns about mounting a campaign to get there. A combination of personal drive and the desire to serve the country and see one's policies in place still makes the job of president of the

Qualifications for the Office of the Presidency

According to the U.S. Constitution, a president must be:

- A natural-born U.S. citizen;
- At least thirty-five years old;
- A U.S. resident for at least fourteen years.

United States an irresistible career move for many people both inside and outside of politics.

Where Do They Come From? The Candidates' Varied Backgrounds

Where do these people come from—these individuals who feel themselves qualified to lead their country and, in a sense, the world? More often than not, they come from other elective offices—governorships, the U.S. Senate, the House of Representatives—where they have shown they can appeal to voters and where they have built a public record of decision making and action on a variety of policy issues.

Because American politics has been dominated by white men for so long, women and minority candidates for the presidency have been few and far between. Notable exceptions include former Democratic candidate Jesse Jackson and, in the 2000 contest, Republican candidate Elizabeth Dole. With more women and minorities running for and winning elective office at the local, state, and national levels, political observers say it's only a matter of time before we have a woman or minority president.

For many years, Congress—and, more specifically, the Senate—was considered the best launching pad for a presidential campaign. The power, the prestige, and the national visibility of a position in Washington, combined with experience dealing with issues from the federal budget to international affairs, made serving in the Senate a good preparation if you had presidential ambitions.

On the Democratic side, recent party nominees who served in the Senate at one time or another include John F.

Kennedy, Hubert Humphrey, George McGovern, and Walter Mondale. Among Republicans, Robert Dole, Richard Nixon, and Barry Goldwater all served in the Senate before launching their presidential bids; Nixon also served as vice president under Dwight Eisenhower.

Over the last two decades, however, the Senate has given way to the governors' mansions as the odds-on source of successful presidential candidates. Three of the last four Presidents—Clinton, Reagan, and Carter—were governors before serving in Washington.

The Perks of the Office

In addition to getting to ride in *Air Force One,* the president receives a salary of $200,000 a year plus $50,000 in expenses (both taxable), $100,000 for travel and entertainment (tax free), and retirement benefits. The work of the president is supported by the federal government's vast executive branch and its approximately 3 million civilian employees, who are organized into 100 departments, agencies, boards, and commissions.

Immediately serving the president are the White House staff, executive offices such as the Council of Economic Advisors and the National Security Council, and the members of the cabinet, which is composed of the heads of the fourteen executive departments: Agriculture, Commerce, Defense, Education, Energy, Health and Human Services, Housing and Urban Development, Interior, Justice, Labor, State, Transportation, Treasury, and Veterans Affairs.

One often-cited reason for the recent influx of former governors is the American public's well-documented disillusionment with Washington in the wake of the Vietnam era and the Watergate scandal in the 1970s. According to this theory, the public grew wary of candidates who had made their names in the nation's capital.

Another factor people point to is that international issues are of less importance to voters in these post–Cold War times. As the top elected officials in their states, governors offer real-world experience dealing with key domestic concerns from education and the environment to balancing budgets and reforming welfare. They also offer very relevant expertise in managing large bureaucracies and staffs.

Running for the Boss's Job: When the Vice President Steps Up

Of course, not all presidential candidates come from the Senate or governorships. The vice presidency is considered an excellent stepping-stone to the nation's highest elective office—and not just because the vice president is first in line for the job if something should happen to the president. The office of the vice presidency offers a candidate the national visibility, the staff resources, and the nationwide contacts he or she needs within the party to lay the groundwork for a successful presidential run.

Democratic presidential candidate Al Gore is only the latest sitting vice president to seek the presidency. George Bush won the office in 1988 after serving for eight years as vice president to Ronald Reagan. Other vice presidents who have

The Line of Succession

In the event that the president dies or is unable to serve out his or her term in office, Congress established a line of succession as follows: vice president; Speaker of the House of Representatives; president pro tempore of the Senate; and the president's cabinet members in the order in which their departments were created, starting with the Secretary of State.

Never in the country's history has the line of succession passed below the vice president.

been elected president after serving in the number-two position include John Adams, Thomas Jefferson, Theodore Roosevelt, Calvin Coolidge, and Richard Nixon.

The one possible drawback of a vice president running for president is that the V.P. is associated, for better or worse, with the record of the president whom he or she served. This means opponents often are able to associate a sitting vice president with the controversies and the unpopular policies of the current administration, and the vice president has a hard time countering the criticism for fear of appearing disloyal.

Political Newcomers: Nonpoliticians in the Running

Does a presidential candidate have to have a record in elective office? No. Many presidential candidates have never won election to any public office but enter the contest with other experiences that they and their supporters feel are qualification enough for the job. President Dwight Eisenhower, for example, rose to fame as supreme commander of the Allied Forces in Europe during World War II.

More recent presidential aspirants who had never served in elective office but who entered the race with other experiences include: Jesse Jackson (civil rights activist); Ross Perot (computer company executive); Steve Forbes (publishing executive); and Elizabeth Dole (former American Red Cross president and U.S. cabinet secretary).

Campaign Strategy, Part I: The Candidates and the Issues

Deciding what issues to focus on—and how to do it—is a major decision for the candidates as they weigh how best to connect with American voters. Many candidates, in fact, select just one or two high-profile issues that will differentiate them from the other contenders in their party. Standing out is key in the early going, when a candidate may face ten or more possible competitors for the party's nomination.

In the 1996 contest for the Republican nomination, Steve Forbes set himself apart from his opponents by advocating a "flat tax" that would establish one low tax rate for all Americans. One of his opponents, broadcast commentator and former White House speechwriter Pat Buchanan, chose the issue of U.S. jobs going overseas; Buchanan's remedy was higher tariffs on imported goods.

More often than not, unique and offbeat proposals such as Buchanan's and Forbes's are crafted more to attract attention to the candidate than to provide a preview of how he or she would govern. After all, any major policy proposal that a presidential candidate suggests would require the support of the Congress after the election. And the more dramatic or radical the proposal, the less likely it is that Congress will agree to it.

As a result, these sorts of far-reaching ideas should be thought of as a candidate's neon signs. They beckon you in so you can check out the candidate and what he or she stands for. But at the same time, it's important to keep in mind that many of these proposals won't make it out the White House door if the candidate is elected.

Campaign Strategy, Part II: Dividing the Electorate

Similarly, many candidates seek to differentiate themselves by making direct appeals to specific segments of the party faithful. On the Republican side, individual candidates often battle for the support of the so-called Christian Right by staking out hard-line positions on issues such as abortion and prayer in schools. Recent examples of such candidates include Christian broadcaster Pat Robertson and, in the 2000 race, Gary Bauer, the former head of the Family Research Council, a conservative group that lobbies Congress on issues from abortion and education to homosexual rights.

On the Democratic side, there is often an early fight to gain the support of the most liberal wing of the party. Democrats who have positioned themselves as the "progressive candidate" in recent elections have included Jesse Jackson, former California Governor Jerry Brown, and U.S. Senator Tom Harkin of Iowa. Senator Paul Wellstone of Minnesota was planning a left-of-center campaign for the presidency in 2000 but dropped out of the race because of health concerns.

Protecting the Candidates

The U.S. Secret Service assumed full-time responsibility for protection of the president after the assassination of President William McKinley in 1901. Presidential aspirants were not offered this security option until sixty-seven years later, when Senator Robert F. Kennedy was shot while campaigning for the Democratic nomination for president.

After Kennedy's assassination, President Lyndon Johnson issued an executive order calling for protection of all announced major candidates for the presidency. Johnson's order later became law, with the provision that candidates could decline protection.

Today, a five-person advisory committee determines whether prospective candidates meet the criteria for Secret Service protection. To qualify, a candidate must:

- Be a declared candidate;
- Have received financial contributions and be likely to qualify for federal matching funds; and
- Conduct an active campaign.

The Secret Service has been known to make exceptions to these criteria. In 1979, for example, Senator Edward Kennedy was given Secret Service protection even though he had not formally declared his candidacy for president.

Often, the candidates making these targeted appeals understand from the start that they have very little hope of winning the presidency. Instead, their goal is to introduce their issues into the campaign, to demonstrate support for their ideas, and, hopefully, to have some influence on the party's stands during the general election campaign and beyond.

The front-running candidates in both parties, by contrast, rarely propose controversial goals or policies that might alienate significant portions of their party's voters and prove a liability during the general election. Rather, a front-runner's goal during the early going and beyond is to get the mainstream of the party behind him or her as the consensus candidate and to demonstrate "electability," or the ability to attract the support of the majority of American voters—Democrats, Republicans, and Independents alike—come November.

The Parties and Other Behind-the-Scenes Powers

The challenge of running a competitive campaign for the U.S. presidency is made easier by the existence of the political parties and other organizations—from the Sierra Club to the National Rifle Association—that support individual candidates and their agendas. Although there are rules governing how they can get involved in a candidate's campaign, the parties and other groups often supplement a candidate's own voter outreach by sponsoring political advertising, publishing campaign materials, and organizing get-out-the-vote drives to get as many sympathetic voters to the polls as possible.

Early History: How the Political Parties Came to Be

The U.S. Constitution has nothing to say about political parties. In fact, the Constitution's framers were resolutely opposed to the formation of political parties in this country. Based on their knowledge of the way things worked in Britain, the framers believed that parties created unnecessary and counterproductive divisions among the nation's leaders, and that voters should be able to judge candidates based on their stands on the issues and not their party affiliations.

Before long, however, early opposition gave way to the political and practical convenience of a party system. People realized that the parties enhanced cooperation between the executive and legislative branches of government and made it easier to coordinate policy making among the different levels of government—from the federal level down to the states, cities, and towns. More important, parties allowed diverse groups of like-minded Americans from throughout the country to come together and have an influence on national policy-making and the election of the president.

Every individual elected to the U.S. presidency since George Washington has run with the support of one of the two major political parties of the time.

The Life of the Parties: The Democrats and Republicans Take Center Stage

From the beginning, American politics has been dominated by two major parties. However, the constituencies and the names of these parties have changed over the years. The

Democratic-Republicans of the Jefferson era were succeeded by the Democrats of President Andrew Jackson's time, and the Federalists who came together during George Washington's presidency eventually became the Whigs, who eventually were incorporated with other groups into the Republican Party under President Lincoln.

How have the parties' constituencies changed? Many observers note that in recent years the Republican party has become increasingly conservative. Although there is a range of opinion within the party, Republicans generally advocate a limited role for the federal government in solving society's ills. Republicans also tend to support lower taxes, cuts in a range of domestic programs from social welfare to environmental protection, and increases in spending for defense.

Despite its origins in the antislavery movement of the 1850s, the Republican party has over the last half century achieved important electoral gains in the South. Some trace the party's transition to Democratic President Lyndon Johnson's embrace in the 1960s of the traditional Republican cause of civil rights, a move that drove conservative Democrats—many of them from the South—into Republican ranks.

The Democrats, for their part, have been identified for much of the twentieth century as the more progressive party, thanks in large part to Democratic President Franklin Roosevelt's New Deal programs designed to alleviate problems caused by the Great Depression. Roosevelt's programs converted large numbers of progressive Republicans into progressive Democrats and laid the foundation for ideological battles that continue to this day about the role of the government in solving problems.

The Two-Party System: Pro and Con

Pro

THE PARTIES HELP VOTERS DECIDE

They help clarify the issues and simplify the choices voters have to make in elections. Without the parties, voters would have to find their way with little help through a confusing maze of issues and candidate positions.

THE PARTIES MAKE GOVERNMENT MORE EFFECTIVE

Parties are often the link among the different branches of the U.S. government and the three levels of government—federal, state, and local. They enable politicians to form coalitions and to get things done.

THE PARTIES MAKE IT EASIER TO RUN FOR OFFICE

Just as parties help the voters, they help candidates by providing an existing base of support and mobilizing voters and party supporters behind a candidacy.

Although President Clinton often was accused by fellow Democrats of betraying the party's bedrock principles—for example, by signing a law to end the federal welfare entitlement—the Democrats generally support a more active gov-

Con

THE PARTIES LIMIT THE CHOICES FOR VOTERS

Because we have only two dominant parties, the parties generally select candidates with the broadest possible appeal. The system discourages campaigning by "fringe" or even remotely controversial candidates.

THE PARTIES PROMOTE DIVISION AND DEADLOCK

Each party is forever seeking political advantage over the other. As a result, candidates and sitting office-holders are under pressure to stick to the "party line" and not to compromise with the other party.

THE PARTIES PROMOTE CORRUPTION

Throughout the nation's history, the political parties have been associated with corrupt practices such as patronage and the awarding of government contracts to party insiders. These practices have subsided in recent decades, but today the parties regularly face criticism for questionable fund-raising practices (see chapter 5 for more).

ernment role in protecting the environment and public health and in ensuring equal opportunity for all citizens.

The Republican and Democratic parties have regularly contested national elections in the United States since the

Civil War. Today, most federal and state officeholders, and many local ones as well, are chosen on a partisan basis.

Party Mechanics: How the Parties Work

The political parties are structured to reflect the U.S. political system, with party organizations at the national, state, and local levels.

THE NATIONAL COMMITTEE

Each of the major political parties is led by a national committee headquartered in Washington, D.C. The key function of the Democratic and Republican national committees today is to raise money to support the party and its candidates.

Other important national committee jobs include planning the party's presidential nominating convention, promoting the election of party candidates at the national level, and coordinating the work of the party at all levels—for example, by creating a unifying message for the party and its candidates.

The national committees are composed of two or more party representatives, including at least one man and one woman, from each state and U.S. territory; the Democrats also include representatives of other groups within the party, including members of Congress, Democratic governors, state and local officials, and party organizations for youth and women.

Appointment to the national committee is considered a high honor and often is a reward for years of service or financial support to the party and its candidates. Some states select national committee members at state party conventions, others select them by a vote of the state party committee, and still others put the selection of national committee members to voters in the party primary.

The chair of the national committee usually is an experienced politician or political professional. He or she is elected by the national committee but often is handpicked for the job by the president or, if the party doesn't hold the presidency, by the party's presidential nominee. As the party's chief spokesperson and administrator, the chair oversees a staff of professionals and consultants in fund-raising, communications, political organizing, and other specialties.

In addition to the national committee, each of the parties has congressional campaign committees that support the party's House and Senate candidates.

THE STATE AND LOCAL PARTIES

The parties also have committees at the state and local levels throughout the country, which play an important role in a presidential campaign. They keep up enthusiasm at the grass roots, distribute campaign literature, and provide staff for headquarters and polling places.

Support from party leaders and volunteers at the state and local levels is considered crucial to the success of a presidential campaign. Not only can they help organize campaign events, but the state and local parties also keep national headquarters informed about the key issues affecting their states and communities, and about which individuals and organizations can help deliver votes.

In addition to supporting the party's presidential candidates, the state committees work to recruit and support statewide candidates, develop a statewide issue agenda for the party, and coordinate the selection of delegates to the national party conventions.

County, city, and town committees, by contrast, recruit and support local candidates and coordinate "on-the-ground" activities such as getting out the vote on Election Day.

Independents' Day: Are the Parties in Decline?

The Democratic and Republican parties may be the dominant political parties in the United States today, but that doesn't mean they have a hammerlock on American politics. In recent years, increasing numbers of Americans have been shunning both major parties and supporting third parties or identifying themselves as Independent.

The percentage of Americans saying they were neither Democrats nor Republicans but Independents rose from 23.3 percent in 1964 to nearly a third—32.9 percent—in 1996. In individual states, the percentage of voters rejecting the major parties often is much higher. For example:

- The state with the highest percentage of voters registering as Independent is Alaska, where more than half of voters shun the major-party labels.
- Placing a close second is Massachusetts, where 49 percent of registered voters identify themselves as Independent.

The loosening of the major parties' hold on the American electorate also can be seen in recent election results. In 1992, billionaire Ross Perot ran for president under the banner of a third political party, United We Stand, and attracted an unprecedented 19 percent of the popular vote—nearly 20 million Americans chose Perot over the major-party candidates, Bill Clinton and George Bush.

The 1998 election of Reform Party candidate and former professional wrestler Jesse "The Body" Ventura as governor of Minnesota is another often-cited example of the electorate's increasing interest in alternatives to the two parties.

Of course, only a very small fraction of elected officials at the national and state levels are unaffiliated with either the Democratic or the Republican party; out of 535 elected

Party Identification in the United States, 1964–1996			
Year	Democrats	Republicans	Independents
1964	52.3	24.8	23.0
1968	46.0	24.5	29.5
1972	41.0	23.8	35.2
1976	40.2	23.0	36.8
1980	41.7	23.0	35.3
1984	37.7	27.6	34.8
1988	35.7	28.0	36.3
1992	35.8	25.5	38.7
1996	39.3	27.8	32.9

SOURCE: National Election Studies, University of Michigan

members of Congress, only 1, Representative Bernard Sanders of Vermont, is Independent.

However, many observers believe that voters these days are focusing more on the candidates than on their party affiliations—and that's making the parties less relevant. One reason is that the advent of television campaigning in the 1960s allowed candidates to appeal directly to the public and over the heads of the political parties, which used to exert much more control over presidential campaigns and the nominating process.

Another explanation of why the Democratic and Republican parties have become less relevant to voters is that it is hard sometimes to distinguish between the two. With the Cold War over, the nation at peace, and our economy in good shape, voters have the impression that there are no

Parties' Spending on the Rise

Their hold on the American electorate may have diminished in recent years, but the political parties are spending record amounts of money in the hope of influencing voters' decisions.

During the 1996 presidential race, the Democratic and Republican parties spent nearly $70 million on advertising aimed at building support for their presidential nominees. The money was provided in unlimited amounts by corporations, labor unions, and other special interests (see chapter 5 for more on the parties' fund-raising activities).

earthshaking issues on which the Democrats and Republicans differ. The result, according to many political observers, is that today's political fights occur only at the margins and around issues that affect few people's lives.

Enter the Special Interests: Independent Groups Step Up Their Campaign Activity

The political parties aren't the only organizations working to influence the outcome of American elections. Recent presidential and congressional races have seen groups such as the Christian Coalition, the AFL-CIO, the American Medical Association, and many others playing an increasingly important—and increasingly aggressive—role in promoting candidates and their ideas and getting Americans to the polls.

Many critics of the current system say that special-interest groups in the United States are exerting unprecedented influence on who is elected to national office. Although independent groups and businesses are forbidden from contributing directly to presidential candidates, they *can* contribute to the political parties and engage in their own outreach to voters through "independent expenditures" and "issue advocacy" advertising.

INDEPENDENT EXPENDITURES

Under current law, there are no limits on how much organizations and businesses can spend on election activities designed to support a particular candidate, as long as those activities are not coordinated with the candidate's campaign.

The only requirement on these "independent expenditures" is that they must be reported to the Federal Election Commission. For example:

> The widget industry can pay for television and radio commercials asking voters to support Candidate X, but only if the widget makers aren't coordinating their activities with Candidate X's campaign. Plus: all of the widget makers' spending on the ads must be reported to the government.

The problem with independent expenditures, critics say, is that they are too loosely regulated and that candidates and their supporters easily can get around the rules.

One group that tried to get around the independent-expenditure rules in 1996, according to the federal government, is the Christian Coalition. Following the election, the FEC filed suit against the group, alleging that the millions of "voters guides" distributed by the coalition in churches and communities throughout the country clearly advocated the election of Republicans over Democrats and therefore should have been reported as independent expenditures.

Issue Advocacy

A study by the Annenberg Public Policy Center at the University of Pennsylvania found that independent organizations spent as much as $150 million on "issue advocacy" advertising during the 1995–96 federal election cycle.

Sponsored by advocates of everything from handgun control to nuclear energy, these ads don't count as independent expenditures because they never explicitly encourage the audience to vote for or against a particular candidate. As a result, spending on issue advocacy commercials doesn't have to be reported, which makes them an increasingly popular way for outside groups to try to influence the outcome of presidential and congressional races without drawing attention to what they are doing. For example:

> Let's say the widget makers didn't want people to know how much they were spending to try to get Candidate X elected over Candidate Y. All they'd have to do would be to sponsor commercials that attack Candidate Y or that talk about what a great person Candidate X is without directly asking people to vote for Candidate X. With an election coming up, it would be pretty obvious to viewers and listeners that the ads were an appeal for their votes, but because the ads qualify as "issue advocacy," the widget industry wouldn't have to make public what it was spending.

Among the big spenders on issue-advocacy advertising in 1996, according to the Annenberg Public Policy Center report, was the AFL-CIO, which spent $35 million on ads supporting President Clinton and labor-friendly congressional candidates throughout the country. A counteroffensive by a coalition of business groups spent $5 million on issue advocacy.

Other organizations sponsoring issue-advocacy commercials in 1996 included the National Abortion and Reproductive Rights Action League, the National Education Association, the National Rifle Association, and the U.S. Chamber of Commerce.

The "issue advocacy loophole," as critics call it, means that groups with a clear stake in the outcome of an election often are sponsoring advertising and other activities designed to support a favored candidate's campaign—and they are doing this with little or no accountability. The Annenberg study calls issue-advocacy commercials "stealth attacks designed to keep the public in the dark."

The result, according to the critics, is more money spent on the election, more thirty-second television and radio ads that clog the airwaves with negative appeals, and more confusion for voters, who often can't figure out who's paying for what commercials—and why. A big problem is that voters have a hard time distinguishing legitimate campaign advertising from the narrow and often negative appeals of independent, single-issue organizations.

Also troubling, according to many observers, is that issue-advocacy campaigns that help a candidate get elected can make that candidate beholden to the special interests who bankrolled the advertising blitz. The organizations sponsoring issue-advocacy commercials counter that they are merely exercising their constitutionally protected right to free speech.

Who's Sponsoring That Ad?

As the presidential campaign season gets under way, television and radio ads will start appearing out of nowhere. Make sure to listen or watch until the end of the ad for the sponsor—and if it's not a candidate's campaign, take the whole thing with a grain of salt: it's probably an independent group with an axe to grind—or with a clear stake in how the election turns out.

The Media

Broadcast television, radio news, and the mainstream newspapers and news magazines have enormous influence on the presidential election process. These pillars of the traditional media are the places where most Americans get the majority of their news and information about the candidates, the issues, and the election.

In recent years, however, Americans have become increasingly disenchanted with the traditional media and their dominant role in American politics. The public's distrust of the old guard—together with the advent of new technologies—has opened the door to new ways for voters to get their election information. From radio talk shows to the Internet and twenty-four-hour cable news channels, the "new media" are becoming increasingly popular as an election resource because they provide unfiltered information about the candidates and the issues, plus a mind-boggling assortment of options for tuning in.

Running for Coverage: The Candidates and the Media

Make no mistake, the traditional media still rule the roost. A modern presidential campaign in the United States is as much a battle for favorable coverage in the mainstream press as it is a battle for votes.

In the early going, for example, the major newspapers and the network news programs can virtually create a presidential front-runner by giving him or her valuable exposure or simply by identifying his or her candidacy as the one to beat. Conversely, if the mainstream media and their political reporters and pundits don't take a candidacy seriously, then raising money and attracting the attention of the voters is an uphill climb.

The bottom line: considering their status as the number-one election information resource for American voters, the media have an important responsibility to dispense their coverage fairly.

The candidates campaign for favorable media attention in a number of different ways. One time-tested technique is to stage events with "good visuals" for the television cameras and news photographers. These can include large crowds enthusiastically waving banners and American flags, or a dramatic backdrop that highlights some of the issues the candidate is talking about—for example, a pristine lake if the topic is the environment or a factory if the candidate is addressing economic issues. Often, a simple meeting between the candidate and voters in a family living room or a local coffee shop is enough to convey the message that this is someone who cares about real people.

Granting exclusive interviews to reporters and news organizations is yet another way in which the candidates court the press. Often, candidates will try to bypass the national media by conducting interviews with local reporters, who are thought to be less jaded and less likely to ask difficult questions.

Thanks to today's satellite technologies, a presidential candidate can sit in a studio in Washington or wherever and conduct back-to-back interviews with television or radio reporters throughout the country. These reporters, in turn, often jump at the chance to offer their viewers or listeners an "exclusive" with one of the contenders for the presidency.

Network Viewership

Despite their declining share of the television news audience, the major networks—ABC, CBS, and NBC—still attract a significant majority of news-hungry Americans. As a result, their coverage of the issues and the candidates can have considerable influence on the course of a presidential campaign.

	Percent Who Watch Regularly
Network News (includes nightly news, news magazines, and morning shows)	57
Cable News (includes CNN, CNBC, MSNBC, and FOX)	40

Source: Pew Research Center for the People and the Press, 1998 Media Consumption Survey, June 1998

The Media Under Fire: What's Wrong with Today's Election Coverage?

Because of their huge influence on the process, the news media often come under fire for how they cover elections. Among the criticisms from voters and politicians alike:

- The media focus too little on the issues and too much on personalities and the "horse race" aspects of elections—who's ahead and who's behind.
- The media have become obsessed with covering—and uncovering—scandals and embarrassing stories involving the nation's elected leaders and candidates for office.
- An entire "talk industry" has developed with politics as its central focus. On cable news channels and radio talk shows, journalists, former government officials, and others routinely offer their analysis and opinions of the latest political goings-on. But whether the "chatfest" actually helps voters is another question. After all, the discussions aren't designed to inform but to draw viewers and listeners in by focusing on controversies, personalities, and scandal.
- Broadcasters face the added charge that their political coverage rarely delves beneath the surface of the issues and instead relies on short, "sound bite" quotes that allow the candidates to avoid saying anything of substance.

Responding to the criticism, many in the news media say they are merely reflecting reality in their campaign reporting. If they report that Candidate X is the front-runner and Candidate Y doesn't have a shot, it's because this is what

Deciphering the Polls

During a presidential election race, the news media often become fixated not on the candidates' ideas or their campaigning but on the latest poll results. Here are a few things to keep in mind as you sort through all the numbers:

- *Who sponsored the poll?* Special-interest organizations often sponsor polls that are designed to place their issues atop the list of voters' concerns.

- *Who was surveyed?* Was it all adults or just likely voters? All parents or parents of school-age kids? These types of things can have a dramatic impact on results.

- *How were the questions worded?* The exact wording of survey questions also can skew the results. For example, if people are asked what issues are important and then are given a list of just five issues to choose from, there's a real possibility that key issues will be left out.

- *When was the survey conducted?* A poll is a snapshot of people's opinions at a specific time. If one candidate is getting favorable attention in the news during the week of the poll, then the numbers are likely to reflect it.

- *What is the margin of error?* Typically, a reputable poll has a margin of error of 5 percent or less. Translation: if the margin of error is 5 percent and one candidate is ahead in the poll by 5 percent, then it's just as likely that the race is a dead heat.

The most important thing to remember about polls, however, is this: the only poll that matters is the official one on Election Day. There's no telling what will happen until the people vote.

party insiders, pollsters, and other experts are telling them; it isn't something the media are making up.

In addition, the focus on personality over policy and on style over substance is driven in large part by what the media believe consumers want. The network news programs are in a constant struggle to increase their ratings, and they fear they'll lose viewers if they produce a ten-minute segment on Medicare reform. Short, snappy pieces about the candidates and the horse race thus become the rule.

The media also defend themselves by saying they are a convenient scapegoat for unsuccessful candidates seeking to explain their poor showing at the polls. During the 1992 election, for example, George Bush and his supporters often claimed that the media were giving the Republican candidate less favorable coverage than his opponent, Bill Clinton. "ANNOY THE MEDIA. VOTE FOR BUSH" became a bumper-sticker slogan and rallying cry for the losing candidate's supporters, while many others claimed that Bush never offered voters a compelling argument for reelecting him to a second term.

The Media Respond: Is Political Coverage Getting Better?

Criticism of the media has had an effect, and it can be seen in how various media organizations have refined their approach to political and issue coverage in recent years.

- They still do their polling and horse-race coverage, but newspapers such as the *Washington Post,* the *New York Times,* and *USA Today* now publish detailed "ad watches" analyzing the validity of claims made in the candidates' radio and television ads.

- A new movement called "civic journalism" or "community journalism" has local newspapers and broadcasters throughout the country pursuing new ways to delve more deeply into issues of concern to the public. Some media organizations are polling the public about what issues concern people most, and then producing special coverage of those topics. Others have expanded their election coverage to include extensive comparisons of local, state, and federal candidates' stands on the issues.

- The television networks now make a point of ignoring the "photo opportunities" staged by the candidates' campaigns and focusing as much as possible on the issues that divide them.

These and other efforts to improve political reporting have not been enough to improve people's perceptions of the media, according to several recent opinion surveys. In a Gallup poll conducted in June 1998, only 34 percent of those surveyed—just over a third—said they had "a great deal" or "quite a lot" of confidence in television news. The percentage reporting high levels of confidence in newspapers was about the same (33 percent). By comparison, 64 percent expressed a high level of confidence in the U.S. military, and 53 percent said the same about the U.S. presidency.

The New Media: Expanding Election Coverage

During the 1990s, several new forms of media entered the picture for voters who had become wary of the dominant role of the mainstream press in the nation's political life. The 1992 presidential election was the first to witness the rise as a political force of the "new media"—a catchall term that has come to include everything from television and radio talk shows to cable television and the Internet.

What was different about 1992? It was the year Bill Clinton appeared on the *Arsenio Hall Show* playing the saxophone, the year CNN and C-SPAN proved once and for all that Americans have an appetite for twenty-four-hour news and public-affairs programming, and the year that presidential campaigns first experimented with using the Internet to communicate with voters.

What unites the many diverse elements of the new media is the way they allow the candidates and their campaigns to bypass the traditional media in an effort to communicate directly with voters. Consider the popularity of radio host Don Imus, whose irreverent, nationally syndicated program has become a required stop for national politicians seeking to connect with voters. Larry King, Rush Limbaugh, and Geraldo Rivera are just a few of the other new media stars.

For the candidates and their campaigns, the new media offer an overwhelming number of ways to tailor messages and appeals to specific voter groups—for example, by appearing on Black Entertainment Television, by connecting with Limbaugh's fifteen million reliably conservative listeners, or by reaching out to younger voters on MTV.

New Media = New Freedom for Voters

For voters, on the other hand, the new media offer a new freedom from reliance on the major newspapers and the broadcast networks, which used to have a lock on what the

American people knew and when they knew it. In particular, the rise of C-SPAN, CNN, FOX, MSNBC, and other cable news networks has allowed Americans to witness for themselves such events as candidate stump speeches, press conferences, and congressional policy debates—events that were previously interpreted for the public by the press.

Dan Balz, a veteran reporter for the *Washington Post,* commented on the situation at a League of Women Voters forum following the 1992 election:

> *Because people now have access to events that in the past could only be seen by reporters, the press is no longer serving as the public's representative. You don't need my story anymore to form a judgment of what you think was important or what you think was interesting . . . Anyone can see the same event.*

By providing voters with a wide range of options for acquiring information about elections and politics, the new media have opened up the political process to voters and offered a more direct line to the candidates and their ideas.

Too Much of a Good Thing? Critiquing the New Media

But the new media is not without its own critics. In particular, the emergence of talk shows such as CNN's *Larry King Live,* which one night might feature a Hollywood celebrity and the next night a candidate for president, has some people worried that journalistic standards are not being met. As *Newsweek* warned in a January 1999 article: "News, public affairs and history itself are morphing into entertainment."

The fear is that television and radio talk shows—together with the speeches and campaign events carried uncut by the cable networks—emphasize congeniality, eloquence, and image over other qualities that Americans should be looking for in a president. And, by providing an end run around seasoned political reporters, they allow candidates to avoid tough media scrutiny of their claims and ideas. The new media, by and large, keep the *candidates* in the driver's seat in terms of what they want to talk about, when they want to talk about it, and with whom.

Tabloid Journalism: POLITICS EXPOSED!

The National Enquirer, The Star, and other tabloid newspapers have been fixtures in supermarket checkout lines for years. But only recently have they become fixtures in the nation's political debate.

After the Monica Lewinsky matter went public in 1998, mainstream news organizations regularly found themselves competing with tabloid reporters to break a story or land an interview with one of the key figures in the events leading up to President Clinton's impeachment trial.

Many people say that tabloids are dragging American politics into the gutter. The mainstream media, by repeating and expanding on the tabloids' reporting, are only making things worse. The only way out is for politicians and voters alike to speak out against the tabloidization of the news—and to pressure newspapers, broadcasters, and others to take the high road when reporting on American politics and government.

Another criticism is that the new media offer an illusion of direct communication with the candidates rather than the real thing. After all, how many people really get through to all the talk shows to ask a candidate a question?

Finding the Best Election Coverage: What You Can Do

What can you do to make sure you're getting the best possible information from the media about the candidates and the issues at stake in the presidential race? The key, according to political experts, is to recognize the pluses and the minuses of the information you receive from all the different types of media. If you aren't getting enough information about the candidates and their positions on the issues from the mainstream press, check out some of the alternatives—for example, by surfing the Internet for more detailed breakdowns of where the candidates stand.

And, if the talk shows and the twenty-four-hour news networks aren't telling you how the candidates' ideas stand up to tougher scrutiny, keep an eye on the morning papers and the nightly news for some good, old-fashioned political reporting.

Last but not least, if nobody seems to be covering the campaign and the issues to your satisfaction, be sure to speak up. Call or write your local newspaper or the local television or radio station and tell them you expect them to do a better job. Casting an informed vote can be tough, and the media have a responsibility to help you decide.

Elections Go Online

The Internet came into its own as a resource for voters and political candidates during the 1996 presidential election. After Republican candidate Lamar Alexander announced his candidacy on America Online, all of the major candidates set up home pages on the World Wide Web. Republican nominee Bob Dole even advertised his Web address during remarks at one of the nationally televised presidential debates.

The Internet's appeal as an election resource rests on the fact that it allows both candidates and voters to completely bypass the traditional media. For candidates, it has become a place to recruit volunteers and post press releases, speeches, biographical information, and issue papers without having to filter everything through other media organizations. For voters, the Internet offers a dizzying number of options for finding out more about the candidates and for researching their positions on issues of concern.

An August 1998 survey by Nielsen Media Research showed that the number of Internet users in the United States was 70.5 million, or about one third of the adult population—and the number was growing fast. Some experts believe that as Internet usage continues to surge and more Americans are able to access election information from their homes, offices, and cars, we'll see an increase in political participation and American democracy will be revived.

Others argue that the Internet's potential in transforming politics and elections in this country is limited by the fact that only a small portion of the electorate uses it as an information resource.

Whatever the case, there are numerous Web sites providing information about the 2000 presidential election, the candidates, and the issues. The following is just an introductory list, and many sites contain additional links that will get you where you want to be:

Browser, Beware!

The openness of the Internet is what makes it a great election-year resource for voters: no matter what kind of information you're looking for, it's a good bet you'll find it. But the Internet's freewheeling, wide-open culture also makes it a place where political scam artists and special interests can seek to influence your vote. A few facts to keep in mind:

- When you're surfing the Web for information about the candidates and the issues, make sure you know the source of that information.

- Some Web sites thrive on rumor and innuendo, others publish patently false stories about the candidates, and still others distort the candidates' views and backgrounds to serve their own political interests.

- During the 1996 presidential campaign, some people set up Web sites that mimicked the sites of individual candidates so they could provide false or misleading information.

The bottom line: Browser, beware! There are plenty of good sites out there that provide helpful information for voters. And the not-so-good ones? Take them off your "Favorites" list.

Web Site Directory

C-SPAN's Road to the White House 2000. Offers video of candidate speeches. *www.c-span.org/guide/executive/rwh/*.

CNN. AllPolitics section offers latest election news and information. *www.cnn.com/ALLPOLITICS*.

The Democracy Network. A collaborative effort of the League of Women Voters and the Center for Governmental Studies, the Democracy Network is an interactive online service that provides one-stop shopping for election and campaign information. *www.dnet.org*.

Democratic National Committee. Official party site offers information on candidates and issues, the convention and party platform, party rules, and more. *www.democrats.org*.

Federal Election Commission. Official site of the government agency that regulates federal campaign finance and election offers information on voter turnout and registration, campaign contributions to individual candidates, and more. *www.fec.gov*.

Grolier Online Presents the American Presidency. Offers age-appropriate information on the presidency, the electoral college, and other issues. *www.grolier.com*.

League of Women Voters. Site provides a wealth of nonpartisan policy information essential to casting an informed vote during election season. Also included are links to state and local sites and information about voter registration. *www.lwv.org*.

MSNBC. Politics section offers latest election-related stories and links to broadcast news reports. *www.msnbc.com/news/politics_front.asp*.

New York Times. White House 2000 page offers election overview, candidate profiles, and the latest political stories from the *Times*. *www.nytimes.com/library/politics/camp/whouse/*.

Project Vote Smart. Offers nonpartisan election and candidate information, plus educational overviews of the powers of the president and other issues. *www.vote-smart.org.*

Policy.com. Online service covers elections and public policy issues. See especially "The Money Chase: Running After Campaign Dollars," March 15, 1999; and "Campaigning on the Internet," October 5, 1998. *www.policy.com.*

PollingReport.com. Nonpartisan site offers updated and archived public opinion polling on elections and public policy. *www.pollingreport.com.*

Republican National Committee. Official party site offers information on candidates and issues, the convention and party platform, party rules, and more. *www.rnc.org.*

Rock the Vote. Site includes youth-oriented information on elections and voting. *www.rockthevote.org.*

Yahoo! Presidential Election section offers election news, plus links to candidate and other sites. *http://www.fullcoverage.yahoo.com/fc/US/Presidential_Election_2000/.*

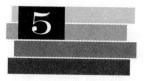

M-O-N-E-Y

Whether you like it or not, cash is king if you're running for president. The conventional wisdom is that a credible candidate for president in 2000 will have to raise $22 million *at a minimum* in order to pay for television advertising, travel, a campaign staff, consultants, and other campaign costs.

And that's just for the primaries! Once the major parties officially name their nominees at the summer conventions, the government gives each of the candidates, along with qualifying Independent and third-party contenders, a set amount of public funds to cover the costs of the fall campaign.

The 1996 presidential election drew new attention to the dominant—and many say unseemly—role of money in American politics today. Together, according to the Federal Election Commission, the campaigns of the two major-party candidates, Bill Clinton and Bob Dole, spent more than $254 million. And, as if that weren't enough, they supplemented their own campaign spending with about $70 million worth of television and radio advertising paid for with special-interest contributions to the Republican and Democratic national committees.

The questionable fund-raising practices that came to light during the 1996 election, combined with the astounding amount of money that was raised and spent, have prompted many Americans to wonder if this is any way to choose a president.

How Did We Get Here? A Short History of Campaign Finance

WATERGATE: THE WAKE-UP CALL

Campaign financing wasn't a major issue in the United States until the 1970s, when the Watergate scandal convinced citizens and lawmakers alike that something needed to be done to stem the flow of special-interest money to politicians and their campaigns.

The introduction of television advertising as a campaign tool in the 1950s and 1960s had dramatically increased the cost of campaigning for public office, and the ensuing scramble for funds left many concerned that American democracy was not being served. Disclosures during the Watergate investigations that corporations and wealthy individuals had made illegal and "laundered" cash contributions to President Richard Nixon's reelection campaign only confirmed people's worst suspicions.

REFORM'S FIRST STEPS

Before the Watergate scandal became public, President Nixon had signed into law the Federal Election Campaign

Act (FECA) of 1971. Among other things, the law required candidates and donors to report their political contributions and spending.

After the new law was revealed as powerless in the face of the Watergate abuses, legislators revisited the campaign finance issue in 1974. The FECA amendments signed into law that year represented the most comprehensive campaign finance legislation ever adopted. Among other things, the law:

- Strengthened requirements for reporting of campaign contributions and spending
- Set strict new limits on contributions and spending in congressional and presidential elections
- Limited individual contributions to $1,000 per presidential or congressional candidate for each primary, general, or runoff election; and capped an individual's total contributions to federal candidates at $25,000 per year
- Created a system of public financing to support the campaigns of presidential candidates who agree to specific contribution and spending limits
- Created an independent agency, the Federal Election Commission, to enforce the new rules.

THE COURT WEIGHS IN

In 1976, the Supreme Court dealt a blow to the 1974 FECA amendments with its decision in *Buckley* v. *Valeo*. The Court's ruling declared that the amendments' mandatory spending limits on congressional campaigns violated the Constitution's free-speech protections. However, the justices let stand the spending limits for presidential candidates who accepted public funds, asserting that these were "voluntary" limits and thus could pass constitutional muster.

The FECA amendments, in other words, didn't *require* presidential candidates to abide by certain spending limits. Rather, the public funds made available by the law were provided only as an *incentive* for the candidates to abide by spending limits, and the candidates were free to say "No thanks."

TINKERING WITH THE LAW

Additional amendments to FECA were passed in 1976 and 1979. The 1976 amendments placed restrictions on spending by political action committees (PACs), which are separate organizations set up by corporations, labor unions, and others to collect and distribute campaign contributions.

The 1979 amendments required reporting of "independent expenditures" by special interests in support of a candidate's campaign and allowed the political parties to spend unlimited amounts of money on "party-building" activities such as voter-registration drives. This last provision created the "soft-money" loophole that has since been used to channel hundreds of millions of dollars from the political parties to their candidates' campaigns (see page 66 for a discussion of soft money).

Public Funding of Presidential Elections: How It Works

Candidates in every presidential election since 1976 have been eligible to receive public funds to cover the costs of their campaigns. The idea behind public funding of presidential elections is to make candidates less dependent on contributions from special interests and wealthy donors. Public money for presidential elections comes from a fund supported by the "taxpayer checkoff" on individual tax returns.

PRIMARY MATCHING FUNDS

During the primaries, candidates can receive partial public funding in the form of matching payments, with the federal government matching all contributions of $250 or less. In other words, if you give $100 to a candidate during the primaries, the federal government will chip in the same amount, but only if the candidate meets certain criteria. These are:

- The candidate must show broad-based public support by receiving at least $5,000 in contributions of $250 or less in twenty or more states.
- The candidate must agree to a national limit on campaign spending for all primary elections. In 1996, the national spending limit per candidate was about $31 million.
- The candidate must agree to spending limits established for each state based on its voting-age population.
- The candidate cannot spend more than $50,000 of his or her own funds on the campaign.

GENERAL ELECTION FUNDING

In addition to the primary matching funds, the presidential nominees of the major parties become eligible for public funding to support *all* campaign costs associated with the general election in the fall. In order to receive the general-election funds, a candidate must limit spending to the amount he or she receives from the federal government while pledging not to accept private contributions for the campaign. In 1996, the two major-party nominees were eligible for general election funding of $61.8 million apiece.

The Self-Funded Campaign

The sky's the limit when a presidential candidate refuses to accept public funds and the accompanying restrictions on campaign contributions and spending. In the 1990s, two candidates said no to public funds while digging into their personal fortunes to cover the costs of their campaigns.

The first was Ross Perot, who in 1992 spent $60 million of his own money on the race, most of it to pay for television time. In 1996, by contrast, Perot decided to accept public matching funds and, as a result, could spend just $50,000 of his own money. Steve Forbes, another wealthy businessman, spent $40 million on his unsuccessful bid to capture the Republican nomination in 1996 and was planning to self-fund his 2000 campaign as well.

Saying no to public financing is not an easy decision, however. A candidate who opts out of the public financing system in 2000 will miss out on up to $15 million in federal funds to support his or her primary campaign.

WHAT ABOUT THIRD-PARTY CANDIDATES?

Third-party candidates also are eligible for public funding to support their general-election campaigns, provided the party's nominee received between 5 and 25 percent of the popular vote in the previous presidential election.

If a third party did not field a candidate last time but is doing so in the current election, its candidate may receive public funding *after* the election is over, but only if he or she receives 5 percent or more of the vote. The amount of public funds available for a third-party candidate is based on the proportion of the popular vote he or she receives.

How Can I Support a Candidate?

Want to support a candidate yourself? Individuals may contribute up to $1,000 to a presidential candidate during the primary election campaign, whether or not the candidate accepts public matching funds. During the general election, however, major-party candidates who have accepted public funding may not accept individual campaign contributions unless the contributions go to the candidate's "compliance fund." This is a fund that a candidate can draw on only to cover legal and accounting costs to comply with the campaign-finance laws.

Third-party candidates are allowed to accept individual contributions of up to $1,000 during both the primary and the general-election campaigns. In other words, it's legal to give them $1,000 twice, whether or not they accept public funding.

Third-party candidate Ross Perot, for example, received about $30 million in public funding to support his 1996 campaign. The amount of public funds made available to Perot was based on his impressive finish in the 1992 election, when he attracted 19 percent of the popular vote.

Getting Around the Rules: Soft Money Isn't Hard to Find

During the 1996 election, the major-party presidential nominees took full advantage of a king-sized loophole in the law to tap their party organizations—and, more important, the parties' major donors—for big bucks. These "soft-money" dollars, in turn, covered the costs of television advertising and other campaign-related activities, over and above what the campaigns paid for themselves.

The political parties receive soft-money gifts from corporations, labor unions, and wealthy individuals. Currently, there are no limits on soft-money contributions or spending, and six-figure donations to the parties from special interests are now common.

In theory, soft money is supposed to be used for "party-building" activities such as voter-registration and get-out-the-vote drives. In reality, however, during the 1990s soft money increasingly has been used to pay for media advertising and other activities supporting the parties' presidential and congressional candidates. By using soft-money contributions, the parties and their candidates have learned that they can easily get around the law's limits on campaign contributions and spending.

Soft-Money Contributions to National Parties Soar in the 1990s

Soft-money contributions to the Democratic and Republican national committees grew at a breakneck pace in the 1990s.

Year	Contributions to Republicans	Contributions to Democrats
1992	$49.8 million	$36.3 million
1996	$138.2 million	$123.9 million

SOURCE: Federal Election Commission

It was the parties' hearty appetite for soft-money contributions that led to some of the most widely reported fundraising excesses of 1996—from White House coffees for major donors to overnight stays in the Lincoln bedroom. The Democratic National Committee has acknowledged that many of the soft-money contributions it collected during the 1996 election were illegal or inappropriate and has returned nearly $3 million in donations. The Republicans also were accused of raising soft-money dollars from questionable sources.

Soft-Money Donors: Who Are They?

During the 1995–96 election cycle, corporations were the single biggest source of soft-money donations for both Democrats and Republicans. Labor unions also were big soft-money donors, giving mostly to Democrats.

Tobacco industry giant Philip Morris was the single largest soft-money contributor in the 1996 election cycle, weigh-

Top Soft-Money Donors, 1995—96

To the Democrats

Joseph E. Seagram & Sons (alcohol/entertainment): $1.171 million

Communication Workers of America (labor): $1.132 million

Walt Disney Co. (media/entertainment): $997,000

American Federation of State, County, and Municipal Employees (labor): $993,000

United Food and Commercial Workers (labor): $714,550

Revlon Group Inc./MacAndrews & Forbes Holdings (cosmetics/holding company): $673,250

MCI Worldcom (telecommunications): $650,203

Lazard Freres & Co. (finance): $637,000

Laborers International Union Of North America (labor): $611,400

Loral Space & Communications (aerospace): $606,500

To the Republicans

Philip Morris Cos. Inc. (tobacco/food/beer): $2.538 million

RJR Nabisco Inc. (tobacco/food): $1.189 million

American Financial Group (insurance): $794,000

Atlantic Richfield Co. (energy): $766,506

News Corporation (media): $744,700

Union Pacific Corporation (transportation): $707,393

Joseph E. Seagram & Sons (alcohol/entertainment): $685,145

Bell Atlantic Corp. (telecommunications): $649,854

Brown and Williamson Tobacco Corp. (tobacco): $635,000

UST Inc. (tobacco): $559,253

SOURCE: Common Cause

ing in with more than $3 million in contributions, mostly to the Republican Party. These donations coincided with a push by tobacco companies for approval of a settlement that would have shielded them from smokers' lawsuits, potentially saving the industry billions of dollars.

Beyond Soft Money: Other Campaign Finance Loopholes

Advocates of campaign finance reform point out that the soft-money loophole is not the only one that allows unregulated amounts of special-interest money to be spent on presidential and congressional elections. Other loopholes include:

INDEPENDENT EXPENDITURES

Corporations, labor unions, and other special interests regularly spend money on advertising and other activities endorsing individual candidates. This is perfectly legal as long as the spending is not coordinated with a candidate's campaign. The problem is it's hard to determine if these expenditures are truly "independent."

ISSUE ADVOCACY

This is advertising designed to build support for a candidate without explicitly telling the audience to vote for the candidate. The problem here is that issue-advocacy commercials allow special-interest groups to escape the reporting requirements they have to abide by when making political contributions or independent expenditures on a candidate's behalf. This has made issue advocacy an increasingly popular way for corporations, la-

Spotlight on Congress

The presidential campaign finance system, believe it or not, is a model of restraint when compared to the rules that govern congressional campaign financing. Because of the Supreme Court's decision in 1976 that *mandatory* spending limits on political campaigns are unconstitutional, there is no ceiling on what a candidate can spend on a race for Congress. In the presidential election, by contrast, the spending limits on the candidates are considered *voluntary* and only apply if the candidate agrees to accept public funds.

The 1998 U.S. Senate contest in New York between former Representative Charles Schumer and Senator Alfonse D'Amato was only the most recent example of how costly many congressional races have become. Schumer won after the candidates spent a total of more than $36 million on their campaigns and put 26,000 television ads on the air.

Advocates of campaign finance reform point out that it's not the amount of money spent on congressional races that's a problem, but where it comes from: special interests with a stake in the policy issues before Congress.

bor unions, and others to try to influence the outcome of federal elections while avoiding detection (see chapter 3 for more).

Cleaning Up Campaigns: Proposals for Reform

The most recent changes to federal campaign finance law were the 1979 amendments to the Federal Election Campaign Act. Considering all that has happened in the twenty years since—exploding campaign costs and the flood of special-interest spending—many people say it's time once and for all for Congress and the president to make some real changes in the way we pay for politics in this country.

Legislation to reform the nation's campaign finance rules, however, has always been a hard sell in Washington. After all, the people who would have to agree to changes in the law got elected under the existing system, so a lot of them think it works just fine. As a result, the numerous reform initiatives proposed in the 1980s and 1990s all went on to defeat.

The excesses of the 1996 election, however, gave new hope to proponents of reform that Congress would act out of sheer disgust to change the current system. During the 105th Congress that ended in 1998, support grew for a compromise approach to reform that would target the most egregious loopholes in the current law by banning soft money and tightening the rules on independent expenditures and issue-advocacy advertising. The Senate blocked action on the reforms, however, after a measure was approved by the House.

During his State of the Union address in January 1999, President Clinton called on Congress to "say yes to a stronger American democracy in the year 2000" by returning yet again to the campaign-finance issue and passing a bill. The jury was still out on whether Congress would heed the president's words, but with the parties already locked in a battle for money for their presidential and congressional races in the year 2000, supporters of reform weren't holding their breath.

Current Campaign Finance Laws

Since Congress started writing rules governing the financing of national elections, a number of provisions have come and gone. The provisions no longer on the books have either been superseded by congressional action or declared unconstitutional by the Supreme Court.

The following provisions regulating presidential campaigns, listed in order from the primary to the general-election campaign season, are still on the books. Each of the provisions is followed by a reference to the year it was passed in its current form by Congress.

Federal regulation: the Federal Election Commission is the federal agency responsible for enforcement of campaign laws (1976).

Disclosure: presidential candidates must file regular reports listing campaign contributions and expenditures (1971). Donors of $200 or more must be listed on the reports (1979). Any organization spending more than $5,000 on campaigns must establish a formal political committee (1979 amendments). Those reports must be filed with the FEC (1976 amendments). Candidates must establish a single organization for their campaigns (1974). The name of the candidate must be listed on campaign materials (1979).

Local Party Expenses: certain expenses of local party organizations, such as get-out-the-vote drives and voter education activities, do not have to be reported (1979). Up to $1,000 in voluntary services, such as lending a home for meetings and lodging, do not have to be reported as contributions (1979).

Independent Expenditures: independent spending of $250 or more must be reported to the FEC (1979). Organizations without formal ties to campaign organizations do not have to adhere to spending limitations (1974).

"Lowest-unit" Rule: to prevent unfair pricing and keep campaign costs down, broadcasters can charge campaigns only as much as they charge other advertising clients for spot commercials (1971).

Political Action Committees (PACs): corporations and labor unions may establish separate units to promote political ends and not be in violation of federal prohibitions on direct contributions (1971).

Taxpayer Checkoff: citizens may indicate on their tax forms that they would like tax money to be put into the Presidential Election Campaign Fund. This fund has been used to help finance nomination and general-election campaigns (1971).

Matching Funds During Primaries: candidates may receive federal matching funds if they raise at least $100,000 in twenty or more states. Each of those states must contribute a total of $5,000 to the candidate in individual donations of $250 or less (1974).

Limits on Contributions: citizens may contribute only $1,000 to each primary or general election campaign, a total of $25,000 to federal candidates overall, and $20,000 to committees of national parties (1976). Candidates may spend only $50,000 of their own or their family's money on their campaigns if they accept federal funding (1976).

Multicandidate Committees: multicandidate committees—most commonly PACs—may contribute only $5,000 per candidate and $15,000 to committees of the national parties (1976).

Continued on next page.

Federal Funding of National Conventions: the parties receive public funding to help cover the costs of their summer conventions (1979).

Spending Limits: candidates receiving federal matching funds may spend limited amounts during the nomination season and other limited amounts in each of the states (state limits are determined by population). The limit is adjusted between elections to account for inflation (1974).

Federal Funding of General Election Campaigns: the federal government offers the nominees of the major parties equal sums of money for the general election campaign. Candidates who accept the money may not raise or use additional campaign funds. The amount of the grant is adjusted each election year according to the inflation rate (1974).

SOURCE: Nelson, Michael, ed., *Congressional Quarterly's Guide to the Presidency,* Washington, DC: Congressional Quarterly, Inc., 1989.

PART II

The Process

Early Action

Legend has it that Lamar Alexander, the former Tennessee governor who ran for the Republican nomination for president in 1996 and lost, wasted no time kicking off his 2000 presidential bid. According to the *Washington Post,* the day after Bob Dole lost to Bill Clinton in the November 1996 election, Alexander was on the phone raising money for his next run.

Presidential campaigns always have started well in advance of the first caucus or party primary. But the 2000 election has given new meaning to the words *early action.* Because of an accelerated primary schedule and the need to raise increasing amounts of campaign cash—all of it in donations of less than $1,000—contenders in the 2000 presidential contest were busy campaigning and raising money earlier than ever before.

As a January 1999 article in the *New York Times* put it: "In many ways, this year [1999] is more crucial than 2000 in determining whom the two parties will nominate."

Laying the Groundwork: Campaigning Unannounced

A presidential campaign begins long before a contender's formal announcement of his or her candidacy. Vice President Al Gore, for example, didn't formally declare he was running for the Democratic party's nomination in 2000 until June 1999, but everybody knew he was gearing up for the race for months and even years before. Similarly, Lamar Alexander was not alone among Republican presidential contenders in getting an early start on the 2000 contest. In 1998, at least eight GOP presidential hopefuls were actively raising money and courting the party faithful to support their 2000 campaigns.

In the earliest stages of the campaign, an "unannounced" presidential candidate tries to build a favorable image in his or her party and throughout the country by making frequent public speeches and appearing at important party functions. It is now common for presidential candidates to start visiting leadoff primary and caucus states such as New Hampshire and Iowa as early as two years or more before voters in those states choose among their parties' contenders. The goals of these early visits are to build name recognition, to make important connections with party leaders, and to create a foundation of support in states that traditionally have set the tone for the primary season.

The Money Chase, Part I: PAC Attack

Another established practice among would-be candidates long before a presidential election is to establish one or more political action committees (PACs). These "leadership

PACs" allow candidates to collect unlimited contributions and not have them count against their presidential fund-raising and spending limits—so long as they haven't officially filed with the Federal Election Commission as candidates for president. As of November 1998, the PAC set up by former Vice President Dan Quayle to support his 2000 presidential bid had raised $1.9 million.

One trick that many presidential candidates now employ in their early fund-raising is to create leadership PACs in states with lax election laws. Unlike PACs established under federal election rules, which are restricted to collecting individual contributions of $5,000 or less, these state-level PACs can collect contributions of any amount. GOP presidential hopeful Steve Forbes, for example, started his PAC (Americans for Hope, Growth and Opportunity) with $100,000 of his own money. At the end of 1998, the PAC already had raised more than $13 million.

Leadership PACs provide candidates with a convenient way around the limits on presidential campaign spending. The ostensible purpose of the PACs is to make contributions to other politicians in their campaigns for office. However, with PAC money a candidate also is able to travel around the country, hire staff and consultants, and develop mailing lists and fund-raising appeals that will form the basis of his or her presidential run. Some candidates even use their PAC money to pay for television and radio commercials in key primary states, even though the primaries are still months away.

PACs have the added benefit of allowing presidential contenders to build goodwill within their parties. By giving money to other candidates, the presidential contenders are distributing chits that they can call in later when they need support among party leaders in key states.

Financial contributions aren't the only way to play the game of you-scratch-my-back-and-I'll-scratch-yours. Would-be presidential contenders also get involved in *campaigning* for candidates for Congress and state offices—flying into a candidate's district or state to make a speech, conduct interviews, or serve as the main attraction at a fund-raising event to benefit the candidate's campaign.

The Money Chase, Part II: The Exploratory Committee

If a presidential candidate feels that he or she has a shot at winning the party nomination based on some of the activities described above, the next step is to file papers with the Federal Election Commission. This allows a candidate to start raising money for polling and other campaign activities that will move him or her closer to a formal announcement.

Filing papers with the FEC usually coincides with an announcement by the candidate that he or she has formed an "exploratory committee" to investigate the possibility of a presidential run. Even if it's clear that the candidate has every intention of running for president, this exploratory committee provides an escape hatch should he or she decide the time's not right to run. Equally important, the announcement of an exploratory committee offers the candidate an early shot of free publicity that can be repeated later on, when the candidate makes it official that he or she is running for president.

In recent elections, the exploratory-committee announcement has become a campaign ritual in and of itself, with the contenders lining up for appearances on television talk shows and Sunday-morning news programs to say they are taking this crucial first step toward running. Representative John Kasich of Ohio, seeking the 2000 Republican presidential nomination, sought to attract even more attention to his announcement by embarking on what his staff called an "Explora-Tour" in early 1999. The trip coincided with Kasich's announcement that he'd created an exploratory committee and took him from his hometown of Columbus, Ohio, to the early battleground states of Iowa and New Hampshire.

From the perspective of the federal officials at the FEC who regulate how candidates finance their campaigns, announcing an exploratory committee is the same thing as announcing a full-fledged campaign for the presidency. The reason is that once a candidate starts raising funds for a presidential bid, everything counts toward the legal limits on contributions and spending, provided the candidate intends to participate in the public financing system. Whether the candidate says he is officially in the race is not an issue.

It used to be that candidates were in no particular hurry to declare their intention to run for president—or even to set up an exploratory committee. All an announcement accomplished was to invite federal scrutiny of the candidate's finances. If the candidate was in a job that allowed him or her to travel the country and talk about issues that might be important in the presidential race, there was little incentive to make a formal declaration of candidacy because the candidate's travel would then have to be paid for by the campaign.

In recent years, however, candidates have realized that the sooner they get started raising the $20 million or more they need to run a credible primary campaign, the better. And to start raising money, they have to file papers with the FEC. With donations for the primaries limited to $1,000 per person, the candidates will need to find more than 20,000 individual donors apiece. And they'll have to do it while their competitors for the party's nomination are knocking on many of the same folks' doors (see chapter 5 for more.)

Competing for Talent: Lining Up Key Advisors and Staff

Another important task in the early going of a presidential campaign is to line up a campaign team. Often, candidates will compete for their party's top strategists and consultants—individuals believed to have the skills and the experience to help ensure the success of a candidate's campaign.

While presidential candidates often rely to some extent on staff members and advisors who have served them in previous positions, it is considered crucial for key members of the team to have national campaign experience, as well as experience and contacts in key primary states.

According to the *Washington Post,* Republican presidential candidate Steve Forbes so wanted Steve Grubbs, the chairman of the Iowa Republican Party, on his 2000 campaign team that he flew Grubbs and his wife to Boston for a dinner on the candidate's 133-foot yacht. Grubbs signed on to

Forbes's team, no doubt providing valuable advice on how to compete in the all-important early caucuses in his home state.

Who's Who: The Campaign Team

Campaign staff members often are referred to as a presidential candidate's "handlers," and they include everyone from a campaign manager and press secretary to the "advance" staff that arranges candidate events just so—with a television-friendly backdrop, a happy, cheering crowd, and, of course, lots of American flags. Some of the key players on a presidential campaign team include the following:

- *Campaign Manager:* oversees the campaign operation.
- *Chief Fund-Raiser:* oversees fundraising and compliance with campaign finance laws.
- *Press Secretary:* manages relations with the news media.
- *Pollster:* conducts polls to track the candidate's support, test the candidate's message, and identify key issues that concern voters.
- *Media Consultant:* produces and buys advertising.

Of course, these are just the top advisors, and a real campaign team includes hundreds, and often thousands, more. Other key players are the campaign volunteers throughout the country who help organize local events, distribute bumper stickers and buttons, and support the candidate at the local level. And don't forget the candidate's "brain trust" advisors—the academics and current and former government officials whom the candidate will call on to help shape his or her policy proposals.

The fact is that a presidential campaign today involves huge numbers of people. A big challenge in the early going is to start building the organization that will put all those people to work as effectively as possible.

Making It Official: The Announcement

In this age of television campaigning, you can bet that a contender for the office of president of the United States is not going to just appear at a press conference on Capitol Hill or somewhere equally unexciting and say, "I'm running."

A presidential candidate's formal announcement often looks like a homecoming rally, with cheering crowds, banners, balloons, and emotional appeals to family, home, and country. More often than not, the candidates return to the places where they were born or grew up so they can show they're normal Americans and haven't forgotten their roots.

Even though the media and the public usually know exactly what will be said at the announcement, the candidate's campaign makes the most of the opportunity to rouse the troops, highlight the candidate's unique qualifications and background, and offer a compelling vision for the country's future.

The announcement provides the candidate with a great opportunity for free publicity, as reporters and television crews from throughout the country draw attention to the candidate's bid for the presidency. Even for long-shot candidates who have little chance of winning any primaries, the announcement provides the "fifteen minutes of fame" that artist Andy Warhol said would someday be achieved by everyone.

Campaign Polling: Fishing for Opinion

For today's presidential candidates, polling has become an indispensable campaign tool from the early phases of the election onward. All of the major candidates employ professional pollsters to keep their fingers on the pulse of public opinion through telephone surveys and other methods. How do candidates use polls?

- To judge their chances of winning.
- To identify issues voters care about.
- To test campaign messages before they are incorporated into advertising and speeches.
- To find out what voter groups—for example, the young, seniors, women, or residents of the Southeast—are most and least likely to support the candidate.
- To figure out whether they are connecting with voters and whether their advertising and other campaigning is having its desired effect—namely, to attract support.

The candidates' polls are rarely made public. They are normally used within the campaigns to help shape and refine campaign strategy, to sharpen the candidates' messages, and to determine what issues he or she should focus on. For example, if polling finds that a candidate's support among women voters is lacking, then the candidate might start to focus on issues that the campaign's polls say women care about.

The bottom line is that for better or worse, what a presidential candidate says in speeches, interviews, and advertising has been thoroughly tested before you, the voter, hear it. In the high-stakes game of presidential politics, it's rare for a candidate to say or do much at all without first consulting the polls (see chapter 4 for more).

After the Early Going: A Winnowing of the Field

By the end of the year preceding the presidential election—for the 2000 election, that means the end of 1999—the field of contenders for the party nominations usually has nar-

The Battle for Endorsements

Presidential candidates crave approval, and endorsements give them exactly that. Throughout the campaign, candidates are constantly battling for the endorsements of key individuals and organizations, including party leaders in key states, celebrities, union and police officials, newspaper editorial writers, and more.

Endorsements by prominent individuals and organizations provide the candidates with an opportunity to step before the news cameras and show that their campaigns are legitimate and that they are attracting support in key places. For voters, endorsements can provide added rationale for supporting a particular candidate—for example, if you're a steelworker and your union has thrown its weight behind Candidate X, or if you're concerned about the environment and one or more environmental groups have endorsed Candidate Y.

But endorsements aren't everything. After all, they are made by people with their own interests, not yours, in mind. A governor who declares his support for a candidate might want a job in the next administration. Who knows? The best approach for voters: don't be swayed too much. The most important endorsement is yours, and you've got to make it on your own.

rowed. If a candidate has failed to attract enough money and other support to mount a competitive race, the best thing to do now is to bow out instead of driving one's campaign further into debt. In the lead-up to the 1996 election, California Governor Pete Wilson announced he was running for the Republican nomination on August 28, 1995, only to bow out of the race just a month later after it became clear that his fund-raising prospects were slim.

No one has even voted yet, and already the winnowing process has begun. Still competing for the nomination are the candidates with the best chances of success—men and women who have raised enough money, attracted enough support from the party faithful, and built enough of a campaign organization to give it a go in the early primaries, now just a few weeks away.

The Primaries
and Caucuses

It used to be that a political party's nominee for president was selected by influential party members at the party's national convention—generally after a lot of wheeling and dealing in smoke-filled rooms. Realizing that this was not a very democratic way to choose a major-party presidential candidate, the Democratic and Republican parties have over the last half century opened up the process to voters. The result is today's often-confusing schedule of primaries and caucuses (see primary season calendar, page 100), which makes voters—and not party leaders—the VIPs in choosing the parties' presidential nominees.

How It Works: Choosing the Delegates

The actual role of the primaries and caucuses is to select delegates to the parties' national conventions over the summer. Even in states where primary voters put a check next to the presidential candidate of their choice, they are actually voting for delegates who support that candidate and will go to the convention representing the voters' interests. In other words, a vote for Candidate X is actually a vote for Delegate Y, who in turn pledges to vote for Candidate X at the party convention.

Because of the primaries and caucuses, the function of today's conventions is not to choose a nominee from out of the blue but simply to ratify the choices that voters already made. The conventions also serve to unite the parties behind their nominees for president and vice president while providing a forum for conducting official party business (see chapter 8 for more on what happens at the party gatherings).

Different states have different ways of selecting delegates to the national conventions. Making it even more confusing, the Republicans and Democrats often do things differently—even in the same state. In recent years, the presidential primary election has become the most common way for voters to have their say. The other main option for choosing delegates is the caucus, where voters meet at the local level to make their preferences known.

Primary Education: What Is a Primary?

In a primary election, voters go to the polls to choose among a party's presidential candidates—or among would-be delegates who have pledged to support specific candidates at the party's national convention. Primaries were conceived early in the twentieth century as one way to take power away from the "party machines" and give the electorate a role in the nominating process. In 2000, the Democrats and Republicans each will hold primary elections in 40 states, in addition to primaries held by both parties in the District of Columbia and Puerto Rico.

PRIMARY TERMINOLOGY

When you're following the news reports and political commentary during primary season, it helps to have an understanding of some of the terms used to describe the different types of primaries:

- *Closed Primary:* A closed primary is the most common type of primary in the United States, with participation restricted to voters who have registered with the party that is sponsoring the election.

- *Open Primary:* In an open primary, a voter shows up at the polls and at that time can choose which party's primary he or she wants to vote in. These types of primaries are not favored by party leaders because they allow voters outside the party to influence the selection of a nominee.

- *Direct Presidential Preference Primary:* In a direct primary, all candidates for a party's presidential nomination are listed on the party ballot. The voters' preferences among the candidates then drive the selection of delegates to the party convention.

- *Indirect Presidential Preference Primary:* An indirect primary asks voters to choose not among the presidential candidates but among would-be convention delegates. Delegates are identified on the ballots as preferring certain candidates or as uncommitted.

- *Binding Primary:* In a binding primary, delegates who are elected by the voters to go to the national conventions agree to support the candidates they are pledged to—at least until it becomes clear that those candidates cannot win the nomination.

- *Proportional Representation Primary:* Delegates to the national conventions are selected on the basis of the proportion of the vote won by the various candidates. In other words, if Candidate X gets 20 percent of the vote in a state or district, then 20 percent of the delegates from that state or district will be committed to Candidate X at the start of the party convention. Proportional representation primaries are much more common than winner-take-all primaries (see below).

- *Winner-Take-All Primary:* Some of the Republican presidential primaries are binding, winner-take-all events, meaning that all of a state's convention delegates must support the presidential candidate who receives the most primary votes in the state. The Democrats have outlawed winner-take-all primaries, preferring proportional representation primaries instead.

For information on the type of primary in your state, contact your local or state Democratic or Republican Party committee, or the local or state elections office. The

National Association of Secretaries of State maintains a Web site (www.nass.org) with links to election information provided by the Secretaries of State in all fifty states.

A Primary Alternative: What's a Caucus?

States that don't hold primaries to select delegates generally convene caucuses as a way to get voters involved in deciding on the party nominees. A caucus is a gathering of voters from the same party at the precinct level; a precinct is the smallest electoral district within a county.

Participants in a caucus vote on party platforms and policies and select delegates to their party's county convention. In a caucus state, anyone who wants to represent his or her state at one of the national conventions must first win election as a county convention delegate at one of the caucuses.

Caucuses generally occur at a set time and date in locations throughout the state; thousands of caucus meetings

Beware the Straw Poll!

In the weeks and months leading up to the primary season, state parties and other organizations often hold "straw polls" that try to measure support for the various candidates among the party faithful. Don't pay much attention to the results: straw polls are unscientific, unofficial surveys and usually reflect the opinions of people who've paid to attend a party function or other meeting. In fact, often a candidate's campaign will try to influence the straw poll results by filling the meeting with his or her supporters.

can be happening all at once. Party rules require caucus dates, times, and locations to be publicized well in advance so voters can plan to attend. The conventional wisdom is that caucuses are won by the best-organized candidates, those who are able to mobilize large numbers of loyal supporters to attend the caucus meetings.

The Early States: Iowa and New Hampshire

Over the last several decades, two states have emerged as the early battlegrounds in the presidential primary season. They are Iowa and New Hampshire, which by custom and party rule hold the first caucuses and primary, respectively, of the campaign season. The voting in Iowa and New Hampshire has proven to be a crucial test for presidential candidates from both parties—so crucial, in fact, that potential candidates can be found in these states years before the election, getting an early jump on the need to schmooze voters and party leaders alike.

Why are these two states so important? Candidates who do well in the Iowa caucuses or the New Hampshire primary get a flood of early media attention and instantly are crowned by the media and others as their parties' front-runners, despite the fact that the overwhelming majority of Americans haven't voted yet. Iowa and New Hampshire often set the tone for the rest of the election, establishing certain candidates as the ones to beat and leaving others in the dust.

All the hype aside, early victories in Iowa and New Hampshire don't necessarily mean a candidate has a lock on the party's nomination. Consider the following early primary winners who went on to defeat:

Year	Candidate	What Happened
1996	Patrick Buchanan	The former White House official won the New Hampshire primary in an upset victory over Bob Dole, but it was Dole who went on to win the Republican nomination.
1992	Paul Tsongas	The former senator beat eventual nominee Bill Clinton in the Democratic New Hampshire primary, appealing to voters as a "favorite son" candidate from neighboring Massachusetts.
1988	Richard Gephardt	The Midwestern congressional leader placed first in the Iowa caucuses in a Democratic nomination fight that was won in the end by Michael Dukakis.
1980	George Bush	The future president beat Ronald Reagan in the Republican Iowa caucuses but had to settle for the vice presidency after Reagan won the party's nomination.

An Accelerated Schedule for 2000

Many observers believe that the influence of Iowa and New Hampshire on the presidential election has diminished in re-

The Expectations Game

The hype surrounding the early primaries often revolves around one thing: expectations. If a candidate who is considered a long shot rises out of the pack to place first or a close second or third, then it's reported in the press as a major victory. On the other hand, if a candidate has achieved "front-runner" status and is expected to win big but doesn't, then it's reported in the media as a setback for the candidate's campaign—and the media pundits and the other candidates all start suggesting that front-runner so-and-so can't win.

Bob Dole, who had been crowned as the clear front-runner in the 1996 Republican contest, attracted only 26 percent of the vote in the Iowa caucuses and was only three points ahead of the next candidate, Pat Buchanan. As a result, the media coverage presented it as though Buchanan had won—he had beaten expectations—while Dole was on the ropes. Dole, of course, recovered over the next few weeks and went on to win the Republican nomination.

cent years. The reason is that increasing numbers of states are moving their primaries ahead on the calendar in a bid to gain more control over the nomination process.

The fact is that many state leaders became jealous of the special attention given by presidential candidates, the media, and the rest of the country to the early primary and caucus states. And so what did they do? They made everything happen sooner.

As recently as 1992, delegate-rich California held its party primaries in June. But in 1996, the state moved its primaries up to March 26, and the 2000 primaries will take place on

March 7, along with several other strategically important states.

These and other states modeled their actions on the move by many Southern states in the 1980s to create a "mega-primary" where voters across the South could make their preferences known. Also known as Super Tuesday, the Southern primary is scheduled for March 14, 2000, and includes Florida, Texas, and many others.

The result of all the shifting dates is a compressed primary and caucus schedule that means the majority of delegates to the 2000 Democratic and Republican nominating conventions will be chosen by the end of March.

Primary Participation: Who Votes in the Primaries?

There is no doubt that the primaries and caucuses have succeeded in getting voters more involved in selecting the major-party presidential nominees. But there are still problems. In fact, many people say we still have a long way to go before we achieve the goal of democratizing the presidential nomination process.

Why? Because voter participation is extremely low in the primaries and caucuses compared to the general election in the fall. In thirty-three primary states surveyed by the Committee for the Study of the American Electorate, just 16.6 percent of eligible voters—roughly one in six—voted in their state's primaries in 1996.

Many people are worried less by the *numbers* of voters in the primary season than by the fact that the primaries and caucuses generally attract certain *types* of voters. Scholars

A Shorter Primary Season: Pro and Con

Pro

It forces early consensus so the parties can rally around their designated nominees. A drawn-out primary season can encourage party infighting as the candidates battle for votes over a period of months. A shortened season, on the other hand, means a front-runner generally emerges by the end of March, and the party can unite behind his or her candidacy and start planning for the general election instead of tearing itself apart.

It places less emphasis on voter sentiment in just one or two states. New Hampshire and Iowa aren't necessarily representative of the country as a whole. And yet these two states have had a significant impact on the country's presidential elections simply by voting early. It might be better to cast a wider net and give more voters and more states a say in shaping the course of the campaign.

(Note: Some observers dispute the notion that a shorter primary season makes Iowa and New Hampshire less important. With less time to learn about the candidates, they suggest, voters elsewhere may be *more likely* to follow the lead of the early primary and caucus states.)

It rewards candidates with the strongest organizations. A primary season where more states vote early benefits candi-

have found, for example, that the average primary voter tends to be slightly better educated, more affluent, and older than the average voter in general elections. Primary voters also are more likely to be interested in a particular candidate dates who have worked hard to build support throughout the country. A shorter primary season thus makes it less likely that a candidate with regional or "fringe" appeal will emerge as the one to beat.

Con

It favors candidates with the most money. It used to be that a presidential candidate could invest heavily in a few early primary states, hoping for a "bounce" from a successful early showing. Today, however, candidates need to campaign from the start in a larger number of larger states. And that puts pressure on the candidates to raise and spend more money.

It means more television ads, less "retail" campaigning. It is impossible for candidates to establish a personal presence in so many states in so little time. The result: more television ads, and less time for the voters to get to know the candidates and vice versa.

It puts unknown candidates at a disadvantage. A handful of early primary elections in less populous states offers relatively unknown candidates an opportunity to show they can connect with voters and run a competitive campaign. This early success, in turn, can attract money and media attention to their campaigns and make them viable contenders for the party nomination.

or to have strong party ties. This could be a problem because it means primary voters might show strong support for a candidate who would not necessarily be supported by the general population.

Tentative Primary/Caucus Schedule — 2000 Presidential Election

The following is a list of 2000 presidential primary and caucus dates for the fifty states, plus the District of Columbia and Puerto Rico, as of July 1999. **Many of these dates are subject to change** as states compete to schedule their primaries and caucuses as early as they can and Iowa and New Hampshire jockey to protect their status as the leadoff caucus state and primary state, respectively.

State	Party	Delegate Selection Method	Date
Alabama	D	Primary	June 6
	R	Primary	June 6
Alaska	D	Caucus	No date set
	R	Caucus	May 19
Arizona	D	Primary	March 10
	R	Primary	February 22
Arkansas	D	Primary	May 23
	R	Primary	May 23
California	D	Primary	March 7
	R	Primary	March 7
Colorado	D	Primary	March 10
	R	Primary	March 10
Connecticut	D	Primary	March 7
	R	Primary	March 7
Delaware	D	Primary	No date set
	R	Primary	No date set
District of Columbia	D	Primary	May 2
	R	Primary	May 2
Florida	D	Primary	March 14
	R	Primary	March 14
Georgia	D	Primary	March 7
	R	Primary	March 7
Hawaii	D	Caucus	March 7
	R	Caucus	May 19
Idaho	D	Caucus	May 23
	R	Primary	May 23
Illinois	D	Primary	March 21
	R	Primary	March 21
Indiana	D	Primary	May 2
	R	Primary	May 2
Iowa	D	Caucus	Date not set
	R	Caucus	Date not set
Kansas	D	Primary	April 4
	R	Primary	April 4
Kentucky	D	Primary	May 23
	R	Primary	May 20
Louisiana	D	Primary	March 14
	R	Caucus	Date not set

State	Party	Delegate Selection Method	Date
Maine	D	Primary	March 7
	R	Primary	March 7
Maryland	D	Primary	March 7
	R	Primary	March 7
Massachusetts	D	Primary	March 7
	R	Primary	March 7
Michigan	D	Primary	Date not set
	R	Primary	February 22
Minnesota	D	Caucus	March 7
	R	Caucus	April 25
Mississippi	D	Primary	March 14
	R	Primary	March 14
Missouri	D	Primary	April 4
	R	Primary	March 7
Montana	D	Primary	June 6
	R	Primary	June 6
Nebraska	D	Primary	May 9
	R	Primary	May 9
Nevada	D	Caucus	March 12
	R	Caucus	May 25
New Hampshire	D	Primary	Date not set
	R	Primary	Date not set
New Jersey	D	Primary	June 6
	R	Primary	June 6
New Mexico	D	Primary	June 6
	R	Primary	June 6
New York	D	Primary	March 7
	R	Primary	March 7
North Carolina	D	Primary	May 2
	R	Primary	May 2
North Dakota	D	Caucus	March 12
	R	Caucus	February 29
Ohio	D	Primary	March 21
	R	Primary	March 7
Oklahoma	D	Primary	March 14
	R	Primary	March 14
Oregon	D	Primary	March 14
	R	Primary	May 16
Pennsylvania	D	Primary	April 25
	R	Primary	April 27
Puerto Rico	D	Primary	March 12
	R	Primary	February 27
Rhode Island	D	Primary	March 7
	R	Primary	March 7
South Carolina	D	Primary	Date not set
	R	Primary	February 19
South Dakota	D	Caucus	Date not set
	R	Caucus	June 6
Tennessee	D	Primary	March 14
	R	Primary	March 14
Texas	D	Primary/Caucus	March 14
	R	Primary	March 14
Utah	D	Primary	March 10
	R	Primary	March 10

Vermont	D	Primary	March 7
	R	Primary	March 7
Virginia	D	Caucus	April 15, 17
	R	Primary	February 29
Washington	D	Primary/Caucus	Date not set
	R	Caucus	June 6
West Virginia	D	Primary	May 9
	R	Primary	May 9
Wisconsin	D	Primary	April 4
	R	Primary	April 4
Wyoming	D	Caucus	March 10
	R	Caucus	March 21

Sources: Democratic National Committee; Republican National Committee. Information as of July 1999.

Caucuses, for their part, attract even fewer voters on a percentage basis than primary elections. And caucus voters, who might have to dedicate an entire evening to appearing at the caucus site for a public discussion of candidates and issues, tend to be even stronger partisans than voters in the party primaries.

Despite these drawbacks, there is widespread agreement that the primaries and caucuses are a definite improvement over the smoke-filled rooms and secret deals of the past. The answer to the problem that the primary and caucus participants might not be representative of the wider population is not necessarily to change the system but to get more voters to show up and make their preferences known.

In other words, more voters need to hear the message that going to the polls in November is not enough. By skipping the primaries and caucuses, they're leaving it to others to decide whom they'll be voting for in the fall.

The Conventions

The national party conventions mark the official turning point in the presidential campaign from the primary season to the general election in the fall. Although it is widely known for months before whom the party will nominate as its presidential nominee, the convention allows the party to put aside any intraparty jockeying and squabbles that occurred during the primaries, unite behind its nominee, and set the tone for the fall offensive.

In recent years, the interest of the parties in staging controversy-free and television-friendly conventions has caused both voters and the media to lose interest in the events. It used to be that conventions could easily turn into high-drama affairs as the parties battled within themselves over key issues, and the selection of the party's nominees for president and vice president wasn't certain until the final voting. But today, the conventions have turned into what one television anchor has called "infomercials" for the national parties. They are events that are scripted with one thing in mind: marketing the party and its candidates to the American electorate.

What's It All About? The Function of the National Conventions

Marketing isn't the only function of the conventions, of course. Without the work done at the conventions, the national parties couldn't exist. In addition to nominating the president and vice president, conventions provide direction to the parties and their national committees about party rules and priorities for the four years between presidential elections (see chapter 3 for more on how the parties work). The conventions are the only time the parties gather at the national level, and so there's business to be done both on and off the convention floor. The major items on the convention agenda:

- *Nominate candidates for president and vice president.* This is the convention function that gets the most attention, even though the party nominees usually are known well in advance. Most often, the role of the national party convention today is merely to *ratify* the choice that the voters made during primary and caucus season by nominating the top vote-getter among the party's presidential contenders. In choosing the vice presidential nominee, delegates generally respect their presidential nominee's judgment and ratify his or her choice of a running mate.

o *Adopt a national party platform.* The platform is a declaration of the party's principles and its positions on important issues confronting the nation. Although it is not
binding on candidates, the platform establishes a tone
and a direction for the party's efforts at all levels of government. "Platform fights" can erupt over the party's
positions on hot-button issues such as trade or abortion,
but the parties generally try to smooth out the differences and encourage compromise in the interest of
demonstrating party unity.

o *Adopt the rules that govern the party for the next four
years.* Like any other large organization, the national
political parties need rules to govern how they function.
The conventions offer a chance to discuss and approve
these rules. Conventions can consider changes in party
rules and procedures on issues from the selection of national convention delegates to the composition of the
party's national committee. Convention delegates also
are called on to elect national committee members and
convention officers, and to decide on rules and procedures for the *next* convention in four years.

The convention also provides an opportunity to accomplish the important task of rallying the party faithful. It is a
chance to recognize all the people who have worked hard
for the party and given their time and money to help it suc-
ceed. And it is a time to try and make sure that the party's
supporters are still behind it and will continue to work for
the party and its candidates during the upcoming election
and beyond.

Who Pays? You Do

The American taxpayer foots a large part of the bill for the national party conventions. Every major-party convention in every presidential election since 1976 has been paid for in part with public funds as a way to reduce special-interest influence on the parties and their candidates.

In 1996, the grants to each party's convention fund from the U.S. Treasury were just over $12 million. In addition, the convention host cities raise money from private sources to cover convention-related costs. But don't think the convention delegates get a free ride. They have to pay their own way to and from the convention and for accommodations while they're there.

The Delegates: Who Are All These People?

Convention delegates used to be a fairly homogeneous group of business and labor leaders, wealthy individuals, and politicians—and most of them were white and male and middle-aged or older. But then in the 1970s and 1980s, the parties opened up the delegate selection process in an effort to populate the conventions with more women, minorities, and young people. The Democrats even went so far as to *require* that each state's delegation to the national convention be equally divided between women and men.

In 2000, the Republican convention will "seat" about 2,200 delegates, and the Democratic convention about double that, or 4,300. Although the state delegations at the Democratic convention are larger than those at the Republican convention, both parties base the number of delegates per state on some combination of the state's population and the relative strength of the party in the state—for example, by looking at how well the party's nominee did in that state in the last presidential election.

As described in chapter 7, convention delegates are selected based on the results of the primaries and caucuses in their states, with most of the delegates coming to the convention pledged to support a specific candidate. In addition, the Democrats have uncommitted "super-delegates" who automatically get a vote at the convention because of their position in the party. Super-delegates include all sitting Democratic governors and members of Congress, plus members of the Democratic National Committee. They account for about one in five of all delegates at the Democratic convention.

Instead of super-delegates, the Republicans award states a specific number of "at-large" delegates of their own choosing. The number of at-large delegates per state varies depending on the relative strength of the party in the state—for example, whether or not the state voted for the Republican candidate in the last presidential election, whether or not it has a Republican governor, and the percentage of Republicans in the state legislature and the state's congressional delegation.

Of course, the delegates aren't the only people at the conventions. There are also hordes of media representatives and television pundits, along with issue advocates, from environmentalists and farmers to labor-union and business representatives, who all want the party to embrace their issues.

You won't see these people on the convention floor, though; their lobbying usually takes place behind the scenes at strategy meetings and after-hours receptions.

The Scripted Convention: A News- and Controversy-Free Event

Until the 1950s, it was common for the parties to have "brokered" conventions, meaning that the nomination was up for grabs. Behind-the-scenes deals were made, votes were traded, and a compromise candidate frequently was chosen from the pack as the nominee.

Since 1952, however, when Republican Dwight Eisenhower and Democrat Adlai Stevenson faced each other in the general election after protracted wheeling and dealing at their party conventions, the nomination fight at both conventions has been a foregone conclusion. The job of today's convention delegates is not to choose the party's standard-bearer but to confirm the choice that voters throughout the country made months before during the primaries and caucuses. Even the vice presidential nominee generally has been selected before the convention starts.

According to the political parties, that's just fine. The way they see it, the fewer surprises the better. Since the dawn of the television age, the conventions have been viewed by the parties as their best chance to connect with a national audience and to articulate what the party stands for. Anything that gets in the way of an orderly, television-friendly presentation of the party and its candidates is unwelcome.

Today's national party conventions are so scripted and stage-managed that they resemble a Broadway show more than they do a political free-for-all. Speakers are chosen based on political considerations, they submit their remarks in advance for review by party officials, key events are sched-

Convention Lowlights

1968 Democratic National Convention
A convention planner's worst nightmare, the 1968 Democratic National Convention in Chicago erupted into chaos when protests over the Vietnam War led to bloody street battles between demonstrators and police.

1972 Democratic National Convention
Even though party strategists had planned for nominee George McGovern to deliver his acceptance speech in prime time (around 10:00 P.M. Eastern Time), a floor dispute preceding the speech lasted well into the early morning. By the time McGovern finally stepped up to the podium, most of the television audience had gone to bed.

1992 Republican National Convention
Patrick Buchanan and other convention speakers drew such a hard line on various cultural and religious issues that it irritated mainstream voters watching at home, who later told pollsters they saw the Republican message as intolerant and exclusionary.

uled for prime time, when the most viewers will be watching on television, and potential controversies are (hopefully) swept under the rug so the show can go on without a hitch.

This doesn't mean the conventions aren't worth watching; voters can actually learn a good deal about a party and its candidates by tuning in. It only means that the conventions should be accepted for what they are: a prime-time television program designed to sell you on the party, its nominee, and its message.

The Role of the Media: The Conventions as News Events

Despite the parties' efforts to make their national conventions more television-friendly, in recent years the television networks have drastically cut back their coverage of the events. The reason has been a lack of real news.

After just two days at the Republican National Convention in San Diego in 1996, Ted Koppel, host of ABC's *Nightline,* announced he was returning home to New York. "This convention is more of an infomercial than a news event," he said. "Nothing surprising has happened. Nothing surprising is anticipated."

Whereas the television networks used to provide "gavel-to-gavel" coverage of the conventions, today they broadcast only selected events such as the nominee's acceptance speech. And they regularly cut away from the convention proceedings to talk about what's happening with their correspondents and expert pundits, or to present their own interviews with party leaders.

Sometimes, the way the media covers today's conventions is a good thing—it can mean the viewers are more informed about what's going on than the actual delegates on the convention floor. But often the networks focus too much on convention politics and don't give voters the information they need to make an informed decision come November—for example, by examining the party platforms and how they differ.

Viewers shouldn't despair if they want to see more of the convention proceedings themselves. The advent of cable news networks such as CNN, C-SPAN, and MSNBC means you're bound to find live convention coverage somewhere. Plus, if you're an Internet user, there are countless Web sites maintained by the media, the parties, and other organizations that feature daily convention coverage and the full text of speeches, along with information about the party platforms, candidate biographies, and more (see chapter 4 for a comprehensive directory of election-related Web sites).

And despite the cold shoulder from the television networks, there is generally plenty of convention coverage in the newspapers and other "traditional media." After all, the national party conventions are the biggest media events of the presidential campaign. In 1996, according to some calculations, media representatives at the Republican National Convention outnumbered the delegates by a ratio of *four to one*.

The downside of having all those reporters and television anchors in one place is that they are constantly trying to scoop the competition and create news when news is generally in short supply. This means that stories with little practical impact on the election and the voters—such as the 1996 resignation during the Democratic National Convention of a top Clinton advisor who was caught with a prostitute—become headline news. And the media attention shifts from covering the issues in the election to covering the latest political dustup.

Convention Highlights: A Viewer's Guide

There's always a lot going on at the national party conventions, but a few key events will give you a good idea of what the party stands for and what the presidential election is all about.

THE KEYNOTE ADDRESS

The keynote address is the first highlight of the convention. Presented by a prominent or up-and-coming politician in the party, the keynote serves to rally the party around a specific set of themes and issues and to convey the party's message in a compelling way to voters watching at home.

What to look for: Often, the selection of the keynoter is as important a statement of the party's goals and direction as the speech itself. The keynoter might represent a state or region that the party feels it needs to capture—for example, the South or California—or perhaps an important segment of the electorate that the party wants to reach, such as women, minorities, or younger voters.

ADOPTION OF THE PARTY PLATFORM

Party platforms often are criticized as having little real impact on the election and the positions of the party's candidates for office. Some have said the platforms are built "to run on, not to stand on." In fact, after the 1996 Republican convention, nominee Bob Dole told reporters that he hadn't even read his party's platform and didn't feel bound by it. Still, the platform offers important clues about where the parties stand on key issues.

What to look for: Platform debates leading up to the convention can spotlight important issues that divide party leaders. Where the platform comes down on hot-button topics from trade and abortion to taxes will provide insights into what factions in the party have the upper hand.

THE NOMINATION OF THE PARTY'S CANDIDATE FOR PRESIDENT

With the platform approved, the attention of the delegates and the media turns to the convention's chief purpose: the nomination of the party's presidential candidate. Generally a foregone conclusion, the nomination nevertheless makes for good television as leaders of the state delegations parade to the microphones to put a plug in for their states and to declare the choices of the voters.

What to look for: Watch for your state delegation's announcement during the roll call of the states to prove that your primary or caucus vote counts. Also, the nominating speeches by prominent party leaders represent the party's first chance to start promoting its presidential nominee and his or her background and priorities to a national audience.

THE NOMINATION OF THE VICE PRESIDENTIAL CANDIDATE

Conventions generally honor the wishes of the presidential nominee in the choice of a running mate. This means the vice presidential candidate is known to all by the time of the roll-call vote, and his or her nomination is a formality.

What to look for: The selection of a vice presidential nominee usually is driven by an interest in balancing the party's ticket for maximum vote-getting potential. A presidential candidate from the Northeast, for example, might select a running mate from the South or West, and a candidate from

The Vice Presidency: More Important than You Think

Think it doesn't matter who's number two on the ticket? Think again. Not only have recent vice presidents played a more active role than their predecessors in policy-making, but as the next in line if something should happen to the president, the vice president had better be ready to lead.

The American public has been reminded again and again that it matters who's vice president. During the twentieth century alone, two presidents have died in office (Roosevelt and Kennedy); two were seriously ill (Wilson and Eisenhower); one resigned (Nixon); one was shot (Reagan); and one faced an impeachment trial in the U.S. Senate (Clinton).

Another reason to pay attention to the vice presidential nominees: the vice presidency is considered the perfect platform for launching a presidential campaign. Al Gore and George Bush are just the most recent examples of vice presidents running for their former bosses' jobs. The bottom line: when Americans elect a vice president, it's a good bet they're electing a future front-runner in the race for the presidency.

the party's liberal or conservative wing might choose someone with more mainstream appeal. This is not always the
case, of course, as when moderate Southerner Bill Clinton
chose another moderate Southerner, Al Gore, as his running
mate in 1992.

THE ACCEPTANCE SPEECHES

It used to be that candidates didn't even go to the party conventions. But Franklin D. Roosevelt broke that tradition and
flew to Chicago in 1932 to accept the Democratic Party
nomination, and both party's nominees have done so since.
Both the vice presidential and the presidential nominees give
acceptance speeches on the convention's final day.

What to look for: The presidential nominee's speech is
considered the most important speech of the campaign, set-
ting the tone for the fall election, laying out issue priorities,
and identifying key differences between the parties.

9

The General Election Campaign

After winning the Republican Party's nomination in 1860, Abraham Lincoln was elected to the presidency without ever leaving his hometown of Springfield, Illinois, and without making a single speech. One hundred years later, Republican nominee Richard Nixon traveled sixty-five thousand miles, made 212 speeches, visited all fifty states—and lost.

The day of the "front porch" presidential campaign that was the custom during Lincoln's time is long gone. Today's general election contest is an elaborate production, with the candidates and their supporters crisscrossing the country and blanketing the airwaves with poll-tested political commercials.

With the primaries and the conventions behind them, the goal of the presidential candidates during the fall is to appeal to as many different kinds of people in as many different ways as possible. To accomplish this in a country where nearly two hundred million individuals are eligible to vote is a staggering task. It requires an effective national organization, enormous discipline on the part of the candidates and their campaigns, and large numbers of staff and volunteers, not to mention a great deal of money.

Campaign Strategy, Part I: A Shift to the Center

The fall brings with it a number of strategic decisions for the candidates and their campaign organizations. But perhaps the most important decision facing the candidates as they approach the general election season is how to refine their message so it resonates with a majority of the American electorate.

Why tinker with a message that worked fine in the primaries? Because in the primaries the candidates were appealing to voters of their own parties, but now they are trying to connect with a much larger audience. This means they need to adopt a more mainstream message, a message with broad appeal beyond the party faithful.

"Shifting to the center," as it is called, is often a tightrope walk for the candidates because they don't want to offend their primary supporters or make it appear as though they are abandoning their earlier commitments. In 1996, for example, Republican nominee Bob Dole entered the fall refusing to make his opposition to abortion a focus of his campaign. Following the GOP convention, he said he would not sign a pledge supporting a constitutional amendment to ban most abortions, and he said he would not use abortion as a "litmus test" in selecting judges. Although the announcements troubled the former Senate majority leader's antiabortion supporters, the goal at that point in the campaign was to increase Dole's appeal among the wider population, which polls showed was more ambivalent about the issue.

Many observers of presidential politics say that the interest in crafting messages and themes with the broadest possible appeal makes the candidates overly cautious in what they say. Bold statements on important policy issues will only antagonize certain segments of the electorate, the thinking goes, so the candidates are content to speak in generalities as much as they can.

One often-noted example of the kind of trouble candidates can get into when they get too specific about what they'd do in office is Democratic nominee Walter Mondale's campaign for the presidency in 1984. Running against the incumbent, Ronald Reagan, Mondale paid the price for taking specific stands on several issues, including a proposal to raise taxes. His loss at the polls served as a warning to future presidential candidates that the less controversial their message, the better.

Of course, the candidates' interest in saying as little as possible about some of the critical issues facing the country is in direct conflict with the voters' need to know the candidates' true beliefs. This is why the presidential debates, media interviews, and other unscripted campaign events are such an important part of the fall campaign—they provide the news media and the voters with a chance to ask direct

What's a Wedge Issue?

A man named Willie Horton became famous during the 1988 presidential campaign as a tragic and misleading symbol of Democratic candidate Michael Dukakis's policies as governor of Massachusetts. While on furlough from a Massachusetts prison, Horton had raped a woman and held her and her husband hostage. Dukakis's opponents used the Horton story to paint the governor as "soft on criminals."

The Willie Horton story is an example of how presidential candidates and their supporters work to identify and take advantage of "wedge issues." These are issues that drive a wedge between segments of the electorate and that create doubts about an opponent's policies and beliefs, even among many of the opponent's supporters. Crime is a perennial wedge issue, with candidates regularly staking out hard-line stands on the death penalty, parole for prisoners, and other topics. Other wedge issues that presidential candidates have used in recent years to appeal to voters' emotions include prayer in schools, flag burning, taxes, and abortion.

and often difficult questions of the candidates about where they stand.

Campaign Strategy, Part II: Targeting a Candidate's Appeal

At the same time that the candidates have to reach out to a broad cross section of the American electorate, they also must decide how to target their campaigning for maximum effect. Because of the limited amounts of time and money available to candidates, it simply isn't possible for them to wage a full-fledged campaign in every state or among all voters. This means that the candidates have to focus on specific states and regions that they feel will be decisive in determining the winner of the election. It also means that the candidates have to target their appearances and their advertising to specific groups of voters.

TARGETING KEY STATES . . .

Under the winner-take-all electoral-college system, a candidate who receives a plurality of votes in a state receives all of that state's electoral votes. Because electoral votes are divided among the states based on their populations, the most highly populated states—such as California, Texas, Florida, Illinois, New York, and Pennsylvania—become the main battlegrounds in the general-election contest.

Candidates devote their energies to the largest states that they feel they have a chance of winning. At the same time, they tend to make only token appearances in states where they are assured of victory while conceding those states where

What's a Swing State?

The candidates generally focus their campaigning on "swing states" where no candidate or party has a lock on the majority of voters, or where large numbers of voters declare themselves as undecided among the presidential contenders.

their chances are slim (see chapter 10 for more on the electoral college system and a chart of electoral votes per state).

. . . AND SWING VOTERS

Just as there are swing states, there are also swing voters—individuals who don't necessarily vote along party lines or whose votes are still up for grabs. With the number of Independent voters on the rise in recent decades, presidential campaigns increasingly have focused on attracting the support of this all-important group.

After all, loyal partisans on both sides are very likely to support their party's candidate no matter what, and it's the Independents who can make the difference in a candidate's election.

Some say the rise of Independent voters explains why recent candidates such as Bill Clinton have emphasized a middle course between the two parties' traditional positions and beliefs (see chapter 3 for more on Independent voting). But it's not just Independent voters whom the candidates are trying to "swing." It's also voters who are registered with the other party but who have shown they don't have a problem crossing party lines.

In the 1980s, for example, much of President Ronald Reagan's success at the ballot box was attributed to "Reagan Democrats." These were Democratic voters—many of them rank-and-file union members—who had become disillusioned with their party and were willing to support the Republican presidential candidate.

. . . WITHOUT IGNORING YOUR BASE

The importance of swing states and swing voters doesn't mean the candidates can ignore their most loyal supporters; in fact, they do so at their peril. For the candidates, the parties, and independent organizations, a major focus as Election Day approaches is to organize comprehensive get-out-the-vote (GOTV) campaigns that bring loyal voters to the polls.

An important target of Democratic GOTV campaigns is minority voters, especially African-Americans and Latinos. For Republicans, Christian conservatives provide a reliable base of support, and a good target for GOTV efforts.

Negative or Not? That Is the Question

One of the major strategy decisions facing a presidential candidate during the general election is whether to "go negative" against an opponent. Going negative doesn't mean critiquing another candidate's ideas and policy prescriptions; back-and-forth debate is an integral part of the campaign process. Rather, going negative means going after a candidate himself or herself—in other words, attacking his or her competence and character.

Under some circumstances, such an approach might be legitimate. But beware. More often than not, negative campaigning is a deliberate effort to steer the debate away from the important issues facing the country.

Campaign Tactics, Part I: The Candidates in Control

Not long ago, the political parties played a major role in orchestrating their nominees' campaigns. But with the rise of the primary system and the increasing importance of television, party regulars lost control of the process, and candidates became increasingly independent. Today's presidential contenders are able to talk directly to the voters through the mass media, instead of having to rely exclusively on their parties to get out the message.

Ever since Dwight Eisenhower ran for the White House in 1952, presidential candidates have created national organizations that are independent of the parties to run their campaigns. The Federal Election Campaign Act, which establishes the rules for presidential campaign financing, actually *requires* candidates to create national organizations to handle campaign contributions and expenditures. As campaigns have grown more complex, these campaign organizations have become more professional, relying on political consultants, media experts, and pollsters to plot strategy and provide information and advice.

Sometimes, a candidate's campaign organization itself makes news—for example, when there is dissension within the ranks, or when someone new is brought in to manage key aspects of the campaign. The media generally jump on stories such as these as an indication that the candidate's campaign is in trouble. And critics inevitably suggest that if the candidate can't manage a presidential campaign, how can he or she manage the country?

A finely tuned and cohesive campaign organization, by contrast, can make the difference in steering a candidate to victory. President Clinton's 1992 campaign—with its relentless focus on the state of the U.S. economy—is regularly cited as a model of how a candidate and his or her organization need to stay disciplined and "on message" if they are to win.

Campaign Tactics, Part II: A Little Help from My Friends

The candidates and their organizations aren't alone in waging their campaigns, however. Despite their declining influence on the process, the political parties still play an important role in promoting their nominees.

In fact, the parties' increasing use of special-interest contributions to pay for political advertisements and other election-related activities has come under fire in recent years. The reason: these contributions provide both the candidates and the parties with an end run around existing limits on campaign contributions and spending (see chapter 5 for more on the parties' fund-raising activities).

Many observers feel that the parties today are not as dominant and controlling a force as in the past, but merely extensions of the candidates' campaign organizations—producing and buying advertising, recruiting volunteers, organizing get-out-the-vote efforts, and launching media campaigns designed to get their nominees elected.

Both the parties and the candidates also receive help in the form of advertising, volunteers, and on-the-ground support

Money Talks

Campaign finance rules have a profound effect on the candidates' strategy for the general election. In fact, one of the first major decisions a campaign organization has to make is whether to accept federal funds and the accompanying limits on campaign contributions and spending, or whether to operate with private financing.

Recently, most candidates have chosen to take advantage of the federal funding option, although funds raised privately by the parties and others are now flowing unchecked into the presidential election (see chapter 5). If a candidate is operating under the federal limits on spending, an important strategic decision is how much of the budget to spend on television and other advertising, and when and where to target it. Because advertising is so expensive, the campaigns have to be careful about how they're spending their ad dollars. The key is to be "on the air" at critical times during the campaign—particularly in the final weeks before the voting—and to target advertising in key states.

from major interest groups such as labor, business, and agriculture (see chapter 3).

Campaign Tactics, Part III: On the Ground and On the Air

Today's presidential candidates essentially wage two campaigns at the same time. The first is on the ground and includes all of the candidate's campaign appearances and speeches, as well as the appearances throughout the country of key supporters, from the candidate's spouse and children to the vice presidential nominee, Hollywood celebrities, and prominent party leaders.

The on-the-ground campaign is tightly controlled by the candidate's campaign organization, with advance teams scoping out locations, rounding up enthusiastic, cheering crowds, and creating compelling visuals for television by placing the candidate before a dramatic backdrop and distributing truckloads of banners, signs, and American flags among the crowd.

The primary goal of the ground campaign is to attract media attention—more specifically, to get the candidate and his or her surrogates on the local television news. Unless it is an enormous event, more people will see the event on the news than in person, and if the television coverage presents the candidate in a favorable light, then the campaign has done its job.

The second campaign in which the candidates are engaged is an on-the-air battle of radio and television commercials. This advertising is the most expensive line item in the campaign budget. The advertising gives the candidates massive nationwide exposure that they couldn't possibly achieve on the ground. It takes the campaign directly into voters' living rooms and allows the candidates to project a fine-tuned, poll-tested image.

The Candidates Face Off: The Presidential Debates

One place on the campaign trail where the candidates are guaranteed to get at least a few difficult questions is at the

How to Get the Most Out of the Debates: A Viewer's Guide

Know the Ground Rules

Most debates impose time limits on candidates' answers. These time limits can be a good thing, ensuring that all candidates have an equal opportunity to respond. But they can also inhibit free exchange if they are too strict or enforced too tightly.

Identify the Candidate's Debate Strategy

Does the candidate speak directly to the issues, provide specifics, and present new policies or information? Or is the candidate being more cautious, perhaps seeking to protect a lead in the opinion polls? Is the candidate spending more time attacking the opponent(s) than explaining his or her own views?

Pay Close Attention when the Candidates Talk About How to Solve Problems

How detailed are their policy prescriptions, or are they trying to keep things vague? Listen carefully to find out how the candidates' approaches on the issues are different.

Think about What Issues Concern You Most—and Listen

Listen carefully to the candidates' answers on the issues you care most about. How do they compare with your own views on those issues? Does it sound like those issues are a priority for the candidates?

Don't Let Appearances Guide Your Reactions

A common criticism of debates is that they are driven by image and appearances. Try to put the candidates' voices, their mannerisms, and their clothes aside and listen for the substance of their answers.

Don't Let the Questioners Off the Hook

Whether it's voters or journalists who are doing the asking, good questions make for a good debate. Are the questions provoking the candidates to address the issues or are they merely inviting scripted answers?

Don't Watch a Debate to Determine a Winner or Loser

The news media often race to determine a victor in the debate, but that doesn't mean you have to, too. The key question is not who won or lost the debate, but which of the candidates you feel would make a better president.

presidential debates. The debates are the only time during the general election campaign when the major contenders appear together to discuss the issues in the election.

Debates provide the candidates with an opportunity to present their views directly to a national audience, without having to pay for the time or filter their message through the media. For voters, debates provide a chance to judge the candidates side by side while they articulate their views.

In 1992, the general election debates for the first time moved away from the traditional "press conference" format, where a panel of journalists asks questions of the candidates with little opportunity for follow-up questions or free exchange. Over the last decade, debate formats have varied, but two formats are now dominant:

- In the *single-moderator debate,* the candidates face questions from a single moderator as opposed to a panel of journalists. The moderator generally is selected by the sponsor of the debate, although the candidates often are given an opportunity to reject moderators they feel might be prejudiced against them. This format is considered an improvement over the more tightly controlled press-conference debate because it allows the moderator to follow up on questions that he or she feels a candidate has not answered satisfactorily.

- In the *town-hall debate,* the candidates face questions from voters in the audience. Generally, the voters are handpicked by the debate sponsor to make sure the live audience is not filled with hard-core partisans and instead reflects the opinions and interests of the wider electorate, including uncommitted voters. Often, the debate sponsor will include *only* uncommitted voters in the audience as a way to ensure that the questions from the audience are intended to elicit information and not to make one candidate or the other look good or bad.

Many candidates, of course, prefer to keep the debates as tightly regulated as possible so they can make a polished and scripted presentation. Negotiations over the number and format of the debates have become a regular feature of the fall campaign season.

In 1988 and 1992, the negotiations between the candidates' campaigns were so strained that they nearly broke down, creating the possibility of no debates at all. But the pressure on the candidates to debate has become intense, and not debating is really not an option because a candidate's opponents will likely make political hay of his or her reluctance to face the voters.

Election Day

On the first Tuesday after the first Monday of November, control of the presidential election finally passes into the hands of the American voter—where it belongs. After all the tireless campaigning by the candidates, all the news coverage, television and radio advertising, and expert punditry, and all of the hard work by the candidate's supporters, it all comes down to this: the voters' decision about which of the candidates they feel is most qualified to lead the nation.

Affirming Your Vote: About the Electoral College

You'd think that the election of the president and vice president would be a relatively simple matter—whoever gets the most votes wins. But it's a little more complicated than that. Instead of providing that the president and vice president should be chosen directly by voters, the U.S. Constitution created an institution called the electoral college that has the final say. The electoral college was one of the many ways in which our founders tried to keep "popular passions" from steering the national government in the wrong direction.

In the beginning, the electoral college had considerable power in making an independent choice among the candidates for president and vice president. But today, the sole function of the electoral college is to confirm the decision made by American voters at the ballot box. In other words, despite the existence of the electoral college, voters still are in the driver's seat in determining who will serve as president. So don't think your vote doesn't count.

A College Education: How Does the Electoral College Work?

Under the Constitution, each state is authorized to choose electors for president and vice president; the number of electors per state is equal to the combined number of U.S. senators and representatives from that state. The electoral college thus includes 535 electors from the states—that's one elector for every member of Congress—plus 3 electors from the District of Columbia for a grand total of 538.

When voters choose a presidential ticket including the presidential and vice presidential candidate, they are actually voting for electors pledged to that ticket. In each state, the ticket that wins a *plurality* of the votes—in other words, more votes than any other candidate—wins all of that state's electors. This winner-take-all system is what drives candidates to focus so intently in their campaigning on states with

large populations and, consequently, large numbers of electors (see chapter 9 for more on campaign strategy).

To be elected to the presidency, a candidate must receive
an absolute majority (270) of the electoral votes. The vice
president is elected by the same indirect, winner-take-all
method, but the electors vote separately for the two offices.

If no presidential candidate receives a majority, the House
of Representatives picks the winner from the top three vote-
getters, with each state's delegation in the House casting
only one vote, regardless of its size. If no vice presidential
candidate receives a majority, the Senate picks the winner
from the top two vote-getters.

The Electoral College: Pro and Con
Pro
IT AIN'T BROKE SO DON'T FIX IT

For the past one hundred years, the electoral college
has functioned without a problem and without much
complaint from the public in every presidential election through two world wars, a major economic depression, and several periods of civil unrest.

IT FOSTERS THE TWO-PARTY SYSTEM

The winner-take-all system generally means that third-
party and Independent candidates get few electoral
votes. As a result, the electoral college inhibits the rise

Continued on next page.

of splinter parties that can contribute to political instability and deadlock. (Note: Some people use this argument *against* the electoral college, saying its bias against third-party and Independent candidates locks them out of the process and inhibits debate.)

It Gives Added Power to Minority Groups

Because it's a winner-take-all system, a relatively small number of voters in a state can make the difference in determining which candidate gets that state's electoral votes. This gives well-organized minority groups a chance to have a profound influence on the election by getting their voters to the polls.

It Promotes a Federal System of Government

The electoral college was designed to reflect each state's choice for the presidency and vice presidency. To abolish it in favor of a nationwide popular election of the president would strike at the very heart of our federal system of government, which reserves important political powers to the states.

Con

It Ignores the Popular Vote

The electoral college doesn't base its decision on the popular vote across the country but on which candidates won which states. As a result, there's a chance that someone could be elected president without receiving the majority of the popular vote. Both Rutherford B. Hayes in 1876 and Benjamin Harrison in 1888 were elected president without winning the popular vote.

IT DISCOURAGES VOTER TURNOUT

Because each state gets the same number of electoral votes regardless of how many people show up at the polls, there is no incentive for the states to encourage voter participation. Also, people are more likely under the electoral college system to feel that their vote doesn't make a difference. Voters might be inclined to skip voting, for example, if it's clear from the news and the polls that Candidate X is bound to win their state.

IT VIOLATES THE ONE-PERSON ONE-VOTE IDEAL

Each state has a minimum of three electors, regardless of the size of its population. This gives residents of the smallest states, which based on their population might otherwise be entitled to just one or two electors, more influence than residents of larger states. Voters in smaller states also would be at an advantage if a presidential election were thrown into the House of Representatives in the event that no candidate received a majority of the electoral vote: because each state's delegation would have one vote, all states have an equal say regardless of

Continued on next page.

population. Two U.S. presidential elections, in 1800 and 1824, have been decided by the House.

IT DOESN'T REQUIRE ELECTORS TO VOTE THE WAY THEY PLEDGED TO

It rarely happens, but there's nothing preventing electors from defecting from the candidate to whom they are pledged. Most recently, in 1988, a Democratic elector voted for Lloyd Bentsen for president instead of Michael Dukakis; Bentsen was Dukakis's running mate. The main danger of "faithless electors" is that the candidate who wins the popular vote could wind up one or two votes short of an electoral college majority, and the election would be thrown to the House of Representatives.

Do We Really Need the Electoral College? Proposals for Change

Over the years, Congress has debated a number of changes in the electoral college system. Most of these would require enactment of a constitutional amendment, although individual states can change their own laws governing how they choose electors.

Some people suggest we keep the electoral college but eliminate the winner-take-all rule so that a state's electors would better reflect the preferences of all of the voters in the state. Under this scenario, a state's electors would either be chosen on a congressional-district basis or simply assigned to the candidates based on the percentage of the popular vote each received in the state. For example, if Candidate X received 20 percent of the popular vote in Arizona, he or she would be awarded 20 percent of the state's electoral votes.

These changes might bring the electoral vote more in line with the popular vote, but voters still would be electing the president indirectly. The electoral college, in other words, would still exist.

Getting rid of the electoral college entirely was the goal of a constitutional amendment advanced during the 1970s by former Senator Birch Bayh of Indiana. Under the plan, candidates for president and vice president would run together in each state and the District of Columbia, and voters would make their choices directly. The team with the most votes would then be declared elected, so long as it received 40 percent or more of the popular vote nationwide. If no team reached the 40 percent minimum, there would be a runoff election between the top two vote-getters.

Direct election of the president along the lines of the Bayh plan would effectively bring the one-person-one-vote principle to presidential elections. Opponents, however, say the possibility of a runoff if no one gets 40 percent of the vote could make the presidential election process even more costly and drawn out than it already is. Following the defeat of the proposed amendment by the Senate in 1979, proposals to reform or abolish the electoral college system have attracted little interest on Capitol Hill.

Tabulating the Outcome: The Results Are In!

Before the advent of television, voting machines, and computerized balloting, it could take days or even weeks for the nation to know whom it had elected president. But today the winner often is known within hours after the polls have closed.

The combination of new election technologies and Election Day polling of the voters by the news media (called "exit polling") has cut into the suspense of an election night. The national networks now begin coverage of election returns while the polls are still open and continue until the results are known, which generally doesn't take very long.

Election results are calculated by precinct. As discussed in chapter 7, a precinct is the smallest electoral district within a county; every voter is assigned to a precinct based on where the voter lives. In most of the 188,000 precincts around the country, voters make their preferences known using voting machines and punchcard ballots; the paper ballots of old have become a rarity outside rural areas. At the end of the day, poll workers deliver the ballots and the voting machine printouts to a central place in the county where the results are officially tabulated and made public.

The use of the voting machines and computerized tabulation of punchcard ballots have dramatically reduced the time it takes to decipher the results. It's still not an incredibly speedy process, however, and the final results for a county or state can take a day or more to compile as the precinct reports come in.

Exit Interviews by the Media: Divining the Results

Eager to report on the election results as soon as possible, the news media years ago came up with a method for projecting a winner while the returns still are coming in, even if only 5 percent or fewer of the precincts have reported their results. The media accomplish this by assigning people to interview voters on their way out of the polling place to find out how they voted.

These exit interviews allow the television networks and major newspapers to track the voting in key precincts whose returns usually parallel the complete returns for their states. Based on the exit interviews, a newscaster often is able to tell viewers which candidate has carried a certain state just minutes after the polls in the state have closed. As the night goes on, the television networks race to identify which candidate has won enough states to give him or her the 270 electoral votes needed to win the election.

Exit polls also allow the media to gauge how the voters feel about the candidates and the key issues in the election. The voters' answers to exit poll questions on a range of election-related topics give the newscasters something to talk about while they're waiting for the next state's polls to close.

Early Projections: Jumping the Gun

Of course, the closer the election, the tougher it is to project a result, and often the networks have to wait awhile to de-

Electoral Votes by State

Total: 538	Needed to Win: 270
California	54
New York	33
Texas	32
Florida	25
Pennsylvania	23
Illinois	22
Ohio	21
Michigan	18
New Jersey	15
North Carolina	14
Virginia	13
Georgia	13
Indiana	12
Massachusetts	12
Missouri	11
Tennessee	11
Wisconsin	11
Washington	11
Maryland	10
Minnesota	10
Louisiana	9
Alabama	9
Kentucky	8
Colorado	8
Connecticut	8
Oklahoma	8

Electoral Votes by State — *Continued*

Total: 538	Needed to Win: 270
South Carolina	8
Arizona	8
Iowa	7
Mississippi	7
Oregon	7
Kansas	6
Arkansas	6
West Virginia	5
Nebraska	5
New Mexico	5
Utah	5
Hawaii	4
Idaho	4
Maine	4
Nevada	4
New Hampshire	4
Rhode Island	4
Montana	3
Alaska	3
Delaware	3
District of Columbia	3
North Dakota	3
South Dakota	3
Vermont	3
Wyoming	3

clare a winner. In 1968 and 1976, the presidential race was too close to call on the night of the election, and the winners—Richard Nixon and Jimmy Carter, respectively—weren't projected until the morning after.

By contrast, Ronald Reagan's 1980 victory over Carter was announced by all the networks before the polls had even closed in the West. This caused some people to wonder if the networks' projections had discouraged some West Coast residents from voting after they heard the election was already decided.

Today, the major broadcast and cable networks generally wait until a state's polls have closed to report election results for that state. But they still are able to project a winner of the presidential election before the polls have closed in all states across the country.

For critics of the networks' early projections, the problem is about more than voters not having their say in the presidential contest. By discouraging people from going to the polls, the early projections also keep voters from registering their opinions on important state and local decisions that are on the ballot.

In spite of the potential problems caused by early projections, the national broadcast and cable networks maintain that their First Amendment rights would be violated by any restrictions on their ability to project an election's winners. So the exit polling and early projections remain a staple of the media's election coverage. And, as a result, the television viewer today knows as much or more about the outcome of the election before he or she goes to bed as it once took weeks to find out.

Making It Official

When the final election results are in, the entire country knows who the next president and vice president will be, but the outcome still has to be made official. In December, the members of the electoral college travel to their state capitals to cast their official electoral votes, sign some necessary documents, and pose for pictures before returning home. When Congress convenes in January, senators and representatives gather for a joint congressional session, and the official results are announced from all the states.

At noon on January 20 following a presidential election, the term of the preceding president ends and that of the incoming president begins. At a formal inauguration ceremony, the Chief Justice of the United States Supreme Court swears in the president and the vice president before members of Congress, government dignitaries, representatives of foreign governments, and important well-wishers, as well as a national television audience.

After an inaugural address and parade, the new president is on the job. The American people have made their choice and are looking to the new president to prove them right.

Bibliography

The American Political Dictionary. 10th ed. New York: Harcourt, Brace & Co., 1996.

Asher, Herbert B. *Presidential Elections and American Politics.* 5th ed. Washington, D.C.: Brooks/Cole Publishing Co., 1997.

Barone, Michael and Grant Ujifusa. *The Almanac of American Politics 2000.* New York: Times Books, 1999.

Corrado, Anthony and Charles M. Firestone, eds. *Elections in Cyberspace: Toward a New Era in American Politics.* Washington, D.C.: The Brookings Institution, 1997.

Federal Election Commission. *About Elections and Voting* (www.fec.gov/pages/electpg.htm). Washington, D.C.: Federal Election Commission, 1996–1999.

League of Women Voters Education Fund. *Focus on the Voter: Lessons from the 1992 Election.* Washington, D.C.: League of Women Voters Education Fund, 1993.

League of Women Voters of California Education Fund. *Choosing the President 1992: A Citizen's Guide to the Electoral Process*. New York: Lyons & Burford, 1992.

Mashek, John W. *Lethargy '96: How the Media Covered a Listless Campaign*. Washington, D.C.: The First Amendment Center, 1997.

The National Election Studies, Center for Political Studies, University of Michigan. *The NES Guide to Public Opinion and Electoral Behavior* (www.umich.edu/~nes/nesguide/nesguide.htm). Ann Arbor, Mich.: University of Michigan, Center for Political Studies, 1995–1998.

Nelson, Michael, ed. *Congressional Quarterly's Guide to the Presidency*. 2nd ed. Washington, D.C.: Congressional Quarterly Inc., 1996.

Sabato, Larry J., ed. *Toward the Millennium: The Elections of 1996*. Needham Heights, Mass.: Allyn & Bacon, 1997.

Smithsonian Institution. *Winning the Vote: How Americans Elect Their President* (September/October 1996 issue of *Art to Zoo*). Washington, D.C.: Smithsonian Institution, 1996.

The Twentieth Century Fund. *Let America Decide: The Report of the Twentieth Century Fund Task Force on Presidential Debates*. New York: Twentieth Century Fund Press, 1995.

The Washington Post. *Campaign Finance Special Report* (www.washingtonpost.com/wp-srv/politics/special/campfin/campfin.htm). Washington, D.C.: The Washington Post, 1998–1999.

Wayne, Stephen J. *The Road to the White House, 1992: The Politics of Presidential Elections*. 4th ed. New York: St. Martin's Press, 1991.

Index